Library of
Davidson College

Christoph Blumhardt

and His Message

R. LeJeune

THE PLOUGH PUBLISHING HOUSE
Woodcrest, Rifton, New York

Christoph Blumhardt and His Message

Title of German original: *Christoph Blumhardt und seine Botschaft*

R. Lejeune, Rotapfel-Verlag, Zurich and Leipzig, 1938

Translated by Hela Ehrlich and Nicoline Maas at the Society of Brothers, Woodcrest, Rifton, N. Y. and published by permission of the author and the Rotapfel-Verlag, Zurich.

Printed by
Lansing-Broas Printing Company, Inc.
1963

Copyright © 1963
Library of Congress Card Catalog No. 63-15816

CONTENTS

Christoph Blumhardt, 1842-1919   5

Christoph Blumhardt's Message:
Talks and Sermons

1 Christ the Lord, *Aug. 1883*   95
2 The Power of God, *Feb. 12, 1886*   96
3 God's Allies, *Apr. 16, 1886*   100
4 Behold, I Make All Things New!
    New Year's Eve 1886   105
5 When God Hid His Face, *Apr. 6, 1887*   116
6 The Lampstand of God's People,
    Apr. 13, 1887   120
7 A New Foundation, *Jan. 14, 1889*   124
8 Our Jehova, *Aug. 1891*   129
9 The Light of the World, *Christmas Eve 1894*   136
10 God's Kingdom, *Jan. 26, 1896*   142
11 People of Zion, *May 3, 1896*   151
12 The Church of Jesus Christ, *June 29, 1897*   157
13 Christ in the Flesh, *Christmas Eve, 1898*   168
14 I Am the Lord, *Feb. 4, 1899*   177
15 Jesus Among the Wretched, *Aug. 19, 1899*   186
16 I Am With You, *Jan. 1, 1910*   197
17 Our Human Right, *Sept. 4, 1910*   208
18 The Savior Is Coming! *Nov. 16, 1913*   220
19 The New Reality, *Mar. 29, 1914*   228

CHRISTOPH BLUMHARDT
1842-1919

TO MANY Blumhardt is as yet little known. It is our purpose to give a first impression of his unique witness; for again and again it is obvious that only a very small circle of people are aware of Blumhardt's significance for our time. Indeed, even people who are seriously interested in the spiritual life of our time hardly know his name. Therefore a short description of Christoph Friedrich Blumhardt's life and work seems desirable. This little volume will fulfil its purpose if as many as possible to whom until now Blumhardt was unknown are led to feel they would like to learn more about his witness and his message to our generation. There is also the larger, four-volume edition* which contains Blumhardt's message in rich abundance. It gives the most exhaustive picture of Blumhardt's life, and conveys the essence of the message which was entrusted to Blumhardt.

Blumhardt's life is of decisive significance for our time. Many may ask themselves how it is possible, then, that such a life has remained hidden from people of our time. We are used to hearing almost daily

---

* Published in German, by R. Lejeune, Rotapfel-Verlag, Erlenbach, Zurich and Leipzig.

everything worth knowing in any way; nor is there a lack of effort to place all "great men" of our time into the public light. Yet Blumhardt's life ran its course very much in quiet and in a certain obscurity. The setting of his work was the secluded Bad Boll * in Württemberg. He had taken over its direction from his father, Johann Christoph Blumhardt (1805-1880). There he held devotions and gave sermons for his household. There he dedicated himself to his guests in discussions and pastoral talks. At times, however, he did also come forward more in public. In the eighties of the last century he often came as a preacher to a number of German and Swiss towns. On such occasions he gathered thousands around his pulpit. Near the turn of the century he spoke in numerous political gatherings in his home county, Württemberg, and was brought even into the legislative assembly of the county by the confidence of the people.

Yet almost more significant than this public activity is the fact that he soon renounced both the church and the political activity in public. He retired completely into the quiet of Bad Boll to work among the relatively small circle of those who came to Boll because of him. For them, this quiet spot had become the birthplace of a new life and a spiritual home. Blumhardt's whole personal nature had nothing of the manner of those great men and famous contemporaries who in our time stand out as "leaders" and are

---

* *Bad Boll*: "Bad" is German for spa. At Bad Boll, an abandoned spa, Blumhardt's father had taken over an old hotel to gather his household and provide room for the many guests, mostly people who came to him for spiritual help.

proclaimed as such by enthused followers. Nothing was further from him than to compete with such human celebrities.

What is essential in Blumhardt is the very fact that he did not want to be anything or represent anything coming from himself. He wanted merely to be a modest tool in the hand of Another. No one could speak more humbly of himself than Blumhardt. He sometimes called himself a poor wretch and a miserable human being. When friends urged him to write the story of his life, he rejected the idea with a smile but with the very seriously meant words, "No one needs to know in the future what kind of a person someone like me was; there is nothing to it." And in thinking of the cause which he served with his whole life, he would sometimes say, "When once the whole of humanity is allowed to come to God, then I would like to be a little mouse and hide in the darkest corner. I shall not want to have anything even as big as a fingernail."

These words indicate how Blumhardt in all his humility was nevertheless clearly aware of the significance of his life. He had a task toward the goal that "the whole of humanity may come to God." He sometimes called himself a witness of "what God wants to become in the world." In the sermons he held in Berlin in the spring of 1888, we find the words, "I am often surprised at how people follow me. Wherever I go, in Germany as well as in Switzerland, people follow me. And at home it is the same; from early morning until late at night I do not have a moment to myself. Why do people come to me? Because I am so devout? Oh, certainly not! Or because I have such a fine house at Boll, with beautiful surroundings and good air? Oh no! There are much finer things of this kind elsewhere. But one thing does bring people here: the Savior is doing something. Of this I boast and I am glad. Deeds of God fall into our life which prove that truly it is not Pastor Blumhardt, giving a fine sermon and seeking followers. No; Blumhardt is nothing and all the people are nothing. Jesus, Jesus is here! This is what attracts people and has lasting worth." Very similarly he expressed it many years later, toward the end of his life. "People often ask, 'Whatever does he have at Boll? What is there?' Actually there is no answer to this except to whisper softly into the ears of those who can understand it, 'The Savior is doing something here; Jesus lives; He does it.'" In a sermon of the same period Blumhardt said, "What are you doing here? Did you come here in order to take walks in the garden and in the woods? No; it is much nicer elsewhere. But you came, perhaps without knowing it, because you expect the kingdom of heaven."

And so it was in fact. The people who came to Blumhardt at the time, to hear his sermons and to seek his help in their spiritual or physical need, felt that they were not simply faced with a man of various human gifts and abilities. They sensed in him one whose talking and whose sermons consisted, like those of the apostles, in "the manifestation of spirit and power."

What Blumhardt once said about the importance

of the apostle Paul fully fits himself: "He was not even important, what we call important. The very fact that he formerly so persecuted the Church proves that he had quite a limited understanding. But God wants a vessel which is not important. What is important in him is not his spirit or his intelligence, not even his knowledge of the Bible. What makes him important is the will of God. Just look into the Bible; there is not one man who is really important himself. Even Moses is not an important man; it is the will of God about him which is important. The life atmosphere about these men is a different one from that of other men and nations." It is the will of God which gave significance to Blumhardt's person. It was this special life atmosphere that people sought and found with him.

In making such comparisons we realize clearly the deep difference between an apostle and a genius, as Kierkegaard pointed out with such passionate emphasis. Nor do we believe that we are guilty of confusing divine calling with human genius. Blumhardt's significance does not lie in his manner and talents, not in his natural being, precisely not in what is meant by the "genius" of a man. It lies rather in what God put into his life, in that to which God called him and elected him. Today many prick up their ears at the message this man proclaimed. They seek in him something they cannot find in any of the so-called great men of our time, in any of the great leaders, in any of the brilliant personalities. In Blumhardt they see not only a gifted person, and in his message not only clever human words. No, they sense in him the man of God. They see him as one entrusted with a word of God to our generation, as one through whom God speaks to us in a new way.

Just like the teaching of the apostles, Blumhardt's message, too, is a witness of what he has experienced. It reminds one very much of the words of the Apostle, when he emphasized at times, "I proclaim what I have seen and touched." When Blumhardt preached, he spoke out of a vision. He himself lived in the powers of the kingdom of God which he proclaimed, and therefore he could say, "One needs to have experienced something of heaven, then one knows what the kingdom of God is." Once when he wrote thoughts which were important to him in a little book for the friends of Bad Boll, he gave it the meaningful title, "Thoughts from the Kingdom of God." This should in no way be taken as something far-fetched or presumptuous. It is childlike and natural to one who knows the source from which he draws everything. Thus he was able to answer a question about the origin of the truth he proclaimed and of the power which went out from him, in quite a simple way, "I have it from God himself." Once Blumhardt talked about his father, saying, "It was not ability, not art, not fluency of speech — it was a power of the Savior that made my father a preacher." By these words he characterized his own manner of preaching. This power of the Savior, through which the "Jesus Christ of yesterday" also shows himself as "the same today," gave Blumhardt's speaking and working its apostolic character.

This also explains the almost Biblical character of Blumhardt's life. The understanding of the Bible was newly opened up to us through Blumhardt. What is more, sacred history stood out anew in its truth and reality through Blumhardt's own life. "We are becoming Biblical again," he could say out of the riches of his experience. His life should at some future time be given a place in that "new Bible" of which he himself often spoke; the new Bible which would tell of God's history among men in post-apostolic times.

There was a curious and meaningful coincidence: Modern liberal theology stripped the image of Christ of all that is miraculous, and cut it down to the "historical Jesus" who in no way breaks through the frame of human nature within the grasp of our reasoning. An Arthur Drews thought he could dissolve the life of Jesus into a mere "myth of Christ." Yet at the very same time Blumhardt, on the basis of marvellous life experiences, witnessed to the wonderful power of victory in Christ, the same power that confronts us so forcefully in the story of the Gospels and in the testimonies of the apostles.

A description of the life of this man of God cannot consist of a kind of biographical outline. The outward course of Blumhardt's life has little to do with the real meaning of his life. Any clinging to biographical data would only lead us away from the essential. We also refrain from describing Blumhardt's personality, his human appearance. Yet it goes without saying that what determined his life also set a stamp on his personality. All those who met him received indelible impressions from this personality. Nevertheless there shall be no further mention here of Blumhardt's person in its individual aspects, but only of the witness of God and of his message to us men. In particular we want to reject quite decisively any attempt to deduce or explain Blumhardt's life and message with the help of psychological analysis or on the basis of church-historical associations. Any such attempt needs must run aground on the intrinsic absurdity of trying to understand from below what in fact comes from above.

Blumhardt's witness did not grow out of his theological studies. He himself made it very plain how little his message was based on intellectual work: "I am not concerned with the study of theology. Only a few years ago I was interested in it because I thought I could learn something from it; but then I gave it up. Now I throw myself into living and experiencing and ask God to talk me out of all this stuff that's in my head." The source of his witness is hinted at in the words, "It is quite a different matter whether one learns or whether one experiences what Jesus is." In a similar connection Blumhardt once said, "If only people had prayed with my father, we would have had a different theology a long time ago." To theologians especially this should give food for thought.

Not even to his steady search in the holy Scriptures does Blumhardt owe his witness. Nevertheless it was certainly significant that from his early childhood on he was familiar with the Bible. He seemed to live more in the Biblical, sacred history than in the outward, everyday world history. Yet precisely he, in whose own life this sacred history again became alive, rose above all mere Biblicism. "Our Bible is in heaven. Not one letter of it is of any use to me unless it is given from above." And if anyone wanted to refute the divine truth thus given to him from above, he was apt to reply to such a Biblicist in a bold way, "The Bible may say what it will — God is greater than the Bible."

Blumhardt always listened to God's word. Over and over again he was allowed to hear a living word of God. Therefore he was able to stand up against the scribes, those learned men who often in the name of "what is written" try to smother God's new words and deeds. As Blumhardt once said of his father, he himself was in fact "born out of what the Scripture calls revelation." To him also "the revelation of God in Christ, on the earth in the past and in the future, and therefore also in the present, remained his deepest concern."

Thus Blumhardt was able to say of the fountain at which the men of the Bible had drunk, "This fountain is the wonderful thing we find through all ages in the history of God's people. It is a strange fountain. It consists of a kind of school into which a man is placed. It is the heavenly school in which God himself is able to speak." At the same time he gave a testimony of himself: "We have been drawing our daily nourishment from this fountain ever since the days of Moettlingen. Our strength is merely the search for a living source and — thank God! — also the finding of this source. Marvellous fountains have run, and we have drunk from them and have also in a way grown through them. Whoever cannot say, 'Our whole life is worth nothing without this source at which Joseph drank and Abraham before him, at which Moses drank, at which the apostles drank, without this source there is nothing' — whoever cannot say this, does not understand us; but neither does he understand the Bible. What is the Bible if one denies this source?"

Another time he spoke of how people generally seek God in their inner life, yet do not find any certainty. "Therefore I looked for another place; or rather, I did not look for it, it was given me. Historically it was given to me by my father, whose experiences pointed me to the fact that we must look for the source from which our own 'I' will emanate as a divine 'I'; this source is the deeds of God. God's deeds run through the whole course of time. They justify us in throwing ourselves into the spheres of God's revelations, where His light radiates and where it is said, 'You are my servant. You are employed by me, you are mine! My deeds show it to you, my words tell you of it.' The source lies in what you see as coming from God, in what has already come with the course of the ages. We must seek it in the words and deeds confirmed by the holy Scriptures, in those words and deeds which have made sacred history throughout the ages. This is now easy for us, for we have God's deeds in the name of Jesus. We can say — allow me to speak

from my Moettlingen-heart, my Bad-Boll-heart —
Jesus is victor! Away with everything else!"

Blumhardt knew that his whole life was placed into this history which runs through the ages, the history of God among men. On the ground of this history he experienced those things which determined his life. Like the men of God in the Bible, he too became a servant and witness of God through revelation, through words of God directed to him and through deeds of God done to him.

The extraordinary history of Moettlingen and Bad Boll began with the experiences of father Blumhardt in Moettlingen. In it the life of the son Blumhardt was cradled. It was not simply human history, not simply a part of ordinary world history. Just like sacred history, it was a part of that history which God works and guides on earth in order to lead men toward His kingdom. "We were born from the kingdom of heaven, from that kingdom of heaven which manifests itself on earth."

At the beginning of this history stand those "days of Moettlingen" of which Blumhardt speaks. Again and again throughout his life he witnessed to the decisive significance of that time. "Moettlingen is our birthplace. In reality we still live there today. Without Moettlingen I would not know where we are. Moettlingen is the soil on which we stand and grow. There the Savior has opened the door which is still open today."

So far I have spoken mostly of "Blumhardt." I have not made a specific distinction between the father Blumhardt who stood in the center of those "days of Moettlingen," and the son who continued that history. This was done with a certain deliberateness; for the father and the son Blumhardt are so much one in what is essential that any arbitrary comparison or distinction of the two would be quite wrong. One cannot even understand the son Blumhardt without the father and his experiences. At the same time, the latter's significance would not have reached its full expression, had not the son continued his father's life and work.

It is fact **one** history which carries the life of the father and of the son, and which unfolds its full meaning more and more as it goes on. In certain pious circles the father Blumhardt is sometimes played off against the freer, "more worldly" son. Where this happens it is basically nothing but the kind of prejudice and narrow-mindedness which is unable to comprehend that God-guided history. The unity which binds the old "Moettlingen" of the father to the new "Bad Boll" of the son has again and again been emphasized by the latter. To a visitor from Moettlingen he said, as a greeting to take back to that town, "Tell them that we carry Moettlingen in our hearts, and that whenever we say 'Bad Boll' we really mean 'Moettlingen.' "

In later years his own way, outwardly seen, led him quite a stretch away from the manner in which his father had worked in the old town of Moettlingen and later also in Bad Boll. He then emphasized the unity of the whole history of Moettlingen and Bad Boll all the more strongly. He always pointed to those days of Moettlingen as the source of this history. For the sake of this innermost connection we must here first of all say something of that "Moettlingen" which was not only outwardly Blumhardt's birthplace, but which in a deeper sense represents the starting point of his life.

* * *

Those "days of Moettlingen" were ushered in by Blumhardt's struggle against the dreadful illness of a parishioner at Moettlingen, Gottliebin Dittus. With good reason Friedrich Zündel, in his biography of Johann Christoph Blumhardt, told the history of this illness and its healing in the chapter significantly headed "The Fight." Behind the sinister illness of this Gottliebin Dittus, Blumhardt recognized the dominion of darkness of which the Bible speaks. In this individual case he recognized how great a power this darkness still exerts over men. But from the Bible he also knew of the God "who has saved us from the dominion of darkness, and who has placed us into the kingdom of His beloved Son."

This kingdom had once shown its power in Jesus Christ through repeated victories over the kingdoms of this world. Now Blumhardt asked himself whether in our days this same kingdom simply had to capitulate to the powers of darkness. He did not simply try to interpret in a pious or profound manner the suffering and bondage that faced him. He did not simply try to console himself somehow about this suffering. He struggled for help and deliverance from it. He saw himself confronted with the deepest question, the question of faith itself: May we take God to be certain and real, even in the face of the hard and dreadful realities of this world? "Who is the Lord? I often had to ask myself this question. And trusting in Him who is the Lord, I felt again and again challenged to go ahead. It must lead to a good end, even if it goes down into the deepest depths; else it is not true that Jesus has crushed the viper's head underfoot."

In the report Blumhardt submitted to the high church authorities we read the important passage, "It became clear to me that something demonic was at work here, and it was painful for me that in such a ghastly thing no counsel or remedy should be found. In these thoughts I was gripped by a kind of anger. I jumped forward, took hold of her [Gottliebin Dittus'] stiff hands, and in her unconscious state called her name loudly into her ear and said, 'Fold your hands and pray: Lord Jesus, help me! We have watched long enough what the devil does; now we want to see what the Lord Jesus can do.' After a few moments she awoke, repeated the words of prayer, and the convulsions stopped, to the great astonishment of those present."

Blumhardt called this the decisive moment which threw him with irresistible power into the activity for this cause. Zündel emphasizes the significance of this first experience: "He dared to face this dark event, instead of just letting it happen in dull resignation or thoughtlessness. He addressed himself directly to God, to the Highest, with a firm conviction, or to Jesus who is raised to the right hand of God, and the Lord answered him immediately by His deed. Here he experienced the merciful, powerful intervention of the Savior, just like the stories he had read in the Bible as a child. He began to see that this is a matter of power, of fight, a task of faith. He sensed that, ultimately, divine redemption reaches into human life only to the degree that there is a faith and a longing for it in mankind."

On the one hand Blumhardt had come to recognize that the world is still in a bad way, is still subjected to its "Prince." On the other hand he was very serious about his faith in the living God who can help, who can loosen the bondage, the God who opposes the kingdoms of this world with the revelation of His kingdom for the redemption of men. "Is there then no other power in the world than that of the devil?" Blumhardt had asked. In contrast to what modern man understands by realism, he represented the genuine, Biblical realism. The latter sees not only the powers and forces of this world as real; it also sees God as real. It believes in the truth and reality of God's kingdom. It trusts in the reality of God and His kingdom and does not yield to the realities of this world. "In such struggles Blumhardt had to recognize that in the present state of God's kingdom the most burning question is that of power. Who is to have the power? The darkness or the Savior? In this fight the Lord wants to triumph through the faith of His Church." (Zündel)

Blumhardt believed in the reality of God's kingdom; and in his wrestling for the power of the Lord it was given to him to experience this reality. The struggle against the powers of darkness, which he carried on for almost two years, ended with a complete victory. The true victor in this struggle was proclaimed in the final outcry of the sick woman, "Jesus is victor! Jesus is victor!" With these words the sickness was overcome for good.

Thirty-five years later, on the anniversary of this final victory, Blumhardt said in a sermon, "That was a personal fight against personalities of the darkness. We struggled for 21 months to see who would win: I in the name of the Lord Jesus Christ, or she in her old rebelliousness against the living God. I remained courageous, trusting in the Lord Jesus. It went through harsh things and I was driven into it to the utmost. The thought of Jesus, the beginner and achiever of faith, kept me strong. In the end even the darkness had to exclaim, Jesus is victor!" **Jesus is victor!** This is Blumhardt's experience in this fight; it determined his whole future life. The son Blumhardt quite rightly called this "Jesus is victor!" the basic experience for his father's future life.

This whole "fight" must also have had its historical aspect. Yet the significance of this story for the history of God among men, and the fruits resulting from this fight, remain independent of historical circumstances. Nothing could be more wrong than to cling to the events with prying curiosity or with arrogant criticism. There is no doubt that this fight represents the initial point for all of Blumhardt's future experiences. These future experiences make up the true history of Moettlingen and actually transport us into a new piece of Bible history. The son Blumhardt, whose whole life stood on the ground of this Moettlingen history, also said with emphasis, "One may judge these experiences as one will; this much remains certain: the gratitude and love of tens of thousands for the deep experience of a new life and new hope for life which grew out of that experience. The mighty power of the healing and life-giving words that came out of Blumhardt's mouth had its roots in that experience and became a reality in the hearts of thousands."

These words indicate that in the fight the new life had merely broken in. This new life was now to unfold in rich abundance. The fight had merely ushered in this whole history, and only in its development did its true meaning and importance become fully revealed. Zündel writes at the end of his description of the fight, "This history is not yet ended; only the dreadful side of it has found an ending. The essential part, the merciful intervention of the Lord, goes forward with august and powerful strides." For Blumhardt himself the fight soon receded completely before the new experiences which were given to him immediately afterwards. He felt pained because people directed their curiosity again and again toward this fight and attributed an independent significance to the outward circumstances which accompanied it. " 'But you know, this isn't Moettlingen,' he said to a friend when almost against his will he handed over his report to the high church authorities. The fight was not what the name Moettlingen called to his mind. The experience upon which he built his great hopes, and which he felt as long as he lived was of great significance for the Christian church, was not the fight but the awakening." (Zündel)

The merciful intervention of the Lord at first showed itself in a movement of repentance which began immediately after the decisive victory. This movement took hold of the whole parish more and more and extended even to the neighboring towns and villages. Crowds of people came to Blumhardt to confess their sins and to seek forgiveness through him. In this way, too, this Moettlingen history proved to be a true piece of God's history. Here the forgiveness of sins was experienced as a living reality, while Protestantism only held to it as a doctrine and Catholicism claimed to possess it as a church institution. Jesus stepped forward as the victor over sin. Zündel, who himself experienced this time of awakening, was reminded "in a very definite way of days we are told about in the New Testament, the days of John the Baptist, the days of the apostles. . . . We felt as though in those days a beam of that radiance which is in the heavenly kingdom of Jesus Christ fell on us."

But it did not end with this movement of repentance. Through the power of forgiveness God's remoteness seemed to be ended and the way made free for further merciful, powerful intervention of the Savior. In the story of the paralytic, Jesus substantiated His power to forgive sins by adding to His words, "Your sins are forgiven you," those others, "Arise, take your bed and go home!" In Moettlingen too, in connection with the movement of repentance, people experienced deeds of help reaching down into the physical domain. Blumhardt did not look for it in any way; he often did not even know about it. Yet innumerable people who heard his sermons or who asked for his pastoral help were healed.

Very many experienced that the Lord is truly the one who "forgives all of your sins and heals all your infirmities." Jesus pointed the doubting John to God's deeds that happened before everyone's eyes: "The blind see, the lame walk, the lepers are cleansed." In such deeds He joyfully recognized the breaking in of God's kingdom. So Blumhardt, too, rightly saw manifestations of the living God, signs of His kingdom, in all that happened through him to innumerable people who sought his help.

Our generation already wanted to relegate the miracle to the realm of legends. Even pious circles thought they must limit miracles to sacred history. Believers and unbelievers no longer seriously counted on them. Yet here they were a fact. Here, where men stood in faith in the kingdom of God and were prepared for the intervention of the Lord, the miracle was recognized and experienced as the truly natural. The miracle consists precisely in the manifestation of God's world in the midst of our human world. We call such manifestations of God's world "miracles" only because our experience limits us to our own world and its order. We encounter so little of God's kingdom. Even the Biblical miracles become strange for us to the point of losing all reality, because we ourselves no longer experience such miracles. Miracles are hard, indeed impossible, to understand when one sees this human world with all its hard facts and iron necessities as the only reality and neither knows nor acknowledges God's world. However, they become understandable, even natural, wherever the faith in the living God and His kingdom breaks through the wall that holds us imprisoned in our earthliness. Then God can come to us and reveal His power among us.

The question of miracles has been much debated in our circles, but it is not a theoretical problem which our intellect could solve in this or that way. On the level of our world and its events, separated from God and closed to Him, it can never be more than a question—answered positively by some in rigid piety, and negatively by others in narrow-minded arrogance — a question which finds its true answer at once so simple and so powerful, wherever God's kingdom breaks in victoriously and unfolds its power and its glory. The miracle, "faith's dearest child," belongs in sacred history, which is God's history among men. This sacred history is in itself the greatest miracle, again and again nourished naturally in a wonderful way from the world of God.

Looking back over those days of Moettlingen with

their fight and their victory, with their awakening and their miracles, Blumhardt once said later on, "It was a great time. Those who saw it and lived through it must admit that these things did not happen by chance. They are a prelude to a much greater time of redemption which is still to come over the whole world, not restricted to one church." — "All the help which through him was poured out over others was to him a projection of the coming kingdom of heaven, a dawning of a new age." (Zündel)

His experiences opened up to him the kingdom of God in the true Biblical sense. It became for him the purpose of all God's deeds among men. He proclaimed again the message of the kingdom of God. For centuries Christendom had not shown any true understanding of his greatest concern of the Bible. Blumhardt opened our eyes to the fact that in the history and message of the Bible it is not a matter of human religions and churches, of cults and dogma, not even of inner peace and personal redemption. It is a matter of the coming of God's kingdom, of God's victory over the whole world, of the fulfilment of His will on earth as in heaven. "To him the kingdom of God was something immensely greater, more eternal and more effective for body and soul than anything he saw in Christianity." (Christoph Blumhardt) "To him the kingdom of God was not fulfilled in the satisfaction of private spiritual needs. He saw its goals as great and as wide as creation itself." (Zündel) It was given to him to experience the manifestations of God's kingdom in the midst of the present-day world and its suffering.

These experiences became all the more meaningful for him as they confirmed the Biblical promise of a new world, a world redeemed of the curse of the fall and restored to its original purpose. Through this "door which the Savior has opened" new light streamed into the world, the light of hope. The early Christian hope of a new coming of the Lord for the perfection of His kingdom had been placed under a bushel for a long time. Thus the world remained in its old darkness and the light of this hope was almost completely extinguished. Blumhardt again placed the light of hope on the lampstand. Significantly, he had the words of the Prophet put up in the church at Moettlingen, "The prophecy will yet be fulfilled in its time and at last will become freely manifest and will not remain hidden. However, if it be delayed, wait for it patiently. It will surely come and not delay."

Blumhardt stands before us mainly as a man of hope. This hope set a stamp on his whole personality. "It was not his orthodoxy, not his knowledge of the Bible, not the clarity of his manner in dealing with people, not his gift of preaching, that distinguished him from other believers. What gave his activity its specific character and made his personality an outstanding one was hope in God, hope for the kingdom. In the strength of this expectation he reached out with his whole person toward the goals which the prophets and apostles had envisioned in all their striving." — "In himself, his church and the whole of Christianity, he saw the possibility of developing toward God's kingdom as he envisioned it. Christianity to him was not a finished religion through which men could be saved. It was a real kingdom and government of God which historically begins, continues and is perfected on earth until God is all in all. The preparing of God's kingdom on earth and the increasing rulership of His will determined all his thinking and acting. It culminated in the cry, Jesus comes, yes, Jesus comes soon!" (Christoph Blumhardt)

At all times Christianity has had preachers of the Christ **who has come.** Unlike these, Blumhardt knew himself called to witness to the Christ **who is to come.**

In the lives of both Blumhardts divine history became evident. The rebirth of early Christian hope and expectation was a decisive element in this history and gave it a significance surpassing that of the Reformation. Blumhardt respected and was grateful for what the Reformation had brought us. Yet he himself visualized "a renewed manifestation of God's power, a renewal of divine and spiritual powers as a continuation of what was given and what happened during the time of the Reformation." — "According to Scripture there is much more for us to learn and to practise than what the Reformers were able to give."

In the teachings of the Reformers and in the symbols set up during the time of the Reformation, Blumhardt missed especially the Biblical expectancy. "They are almost completely silent about the coming of the Lord, and do not lead toward an expectation of it. Yet we should be 'like men who are waiting for their Lord.'" Today, the Christian religion and church are mortally threatened by the spirits and powers of the old world. Nevertheless, many Christians see the remedy in a return to the old confessions of the Reformation, instead of opposing the faith in Caesar and his human kingdom by trusting in Christ and in the kingdom of God for which He has opened the way. Blumhardt warned us saying, "To insist on symbols, not wanting to go further than they lead, is very dangerous." This is a very important point for us.

As a man of hope Blumhardt found an attitude toward the world quite different from the general attitude of Christianity in our time. So many Christians like to justify and glorify the world as willed by God, and thoughtlessly speak of a "divine world order." Blumhardt however recognized that this world is not yet God's, that it will yet have to become His.

He saw the world in all its temporariness, and not as something given once for all, which we have to accept in pious resignation. "It is much easier to get used to a resignation to God's will, than to push aside the barriers which hold up God's help." In the light of Biblical expectation the world appeared to him as the old creation which has to yield to the new one as the night yields to the dawning day. The redemption Christ brought to the world is not yet consummated. For us as for the Christians of the beginning time it is a matter of "waiting for a new heaven and a new earth where justice will dwell according to God's promise."

He who begain the great work of redemption

among us told us to pray, "Thy kingdom come! Thy will be done on earth as in heaven! Deliver us from evil!" He exhorted us to "be as men who wait for their Lord!" Until this end which Christ will prepare for our world has come, we can only wait and pray. We may do it in the certain hope that He who has begun this work will also consummate it.

One of the most important of the songs written by Blumhardt — which differ from the majority of our church songs in that their true Biblical spirit embraces the whole world with its hope — begins with the meaningful words, "Christ's victory remains forever sure; the whole world will be His!" Until then many Christians may have sung, "The whole world **is** His." This gave a deceptive shine of glorification to the world and hindered the expectation of further victories of God on earth. Blumhardt however spoke of God's coming into His own on the earth. He placed himself, with his whole faith and hope, fighting and working, into the service of this coming and became a powerful "witness of the future of mankind according to God's promise; a future that holds the magnificent end of what exists today, and the blissful beginning of a new creation." These words were said of the father by the son.

There is much fatalism in the basic attitude taken by Christians nowadays toward the world situation and world events. True, this fatalism is glossed over to some extent by a certain pious manner of looking at things or expressing oneself. Those who have recognized this clearly will be able to estimate the deep change heralded by the rebirth of Christian hope and expectation.

In the past the early Christian expectation of God's kingdom broke through the hopeless fatalism of heathen antiquity and brought to the Western world a salutary element of unrest. Similarly, the renewal of Christian hope is called to overcome this new pessimism which yields to the powers and authorities of the world and despairs of the victory of God's cause on earth. Nevertheless, Blumhardt's hope for the coming of God's kingdom had nothing to do with the kind of optimism that flourishes in our time, which trusts in human progress and spontaneous evolution. Blumhardt was far from such naive optimism. He saw too deeply into the unredeemed condition of the world; he wrestled with the powers of evil. Again and again he experienced the power of victory of the living Christ; on this alone he based his hope.

Blumhardt was at all times aware of the fact that only the history of God can lead men out of their own history. He knew that a new intervention of God, a new revelation, is needed again and again. His expectation found its strongest and truest expression in his hope for a new outpouring of the Holy Spirit, which alone can lead men forward into times of fulfilment.

Blumhardt also expressed in a song this attitude of faith and powerful hope for the victory of Christ's cause. The song was given to him during the days of

Moettlingen. The congregation at Moettlingen and at Bad Boll sang it often for many decades with ever new and living faith:

> Jesus is victorious king,
> Who o'er all His foes has conquered.
> Jesus, soon the world will fall
> At His feet, by love o'erpowered.
> Jesus leads us with His might
> From the darkness to radiant light.

* * *

Moettlingen, the scene of battle and victory, with its rich experiences of a merciful, powerful intervention of the Lord, and its living hope for the coming of God's kingdom, was the soil on which the son Christoph Blumhardt stood and grew.

Born on June 1, 1842, during the first period of the "fight", he grew up in an atmosphere of the tangible proximity of God. It was not surprising, therefore, that the amazing experiences of his father engraved themselves quite early on the wide open soul of the child. He was deeply impressed by Jesus the Victor. We see the boy already at the age of 13 carefully copying out his father's sermons. He himself later wrote how he looked up to his father's innermost being, as it came to him through the latter's sermons and devotions. Until he was 16 his father taught him all the subjects needed for further studies. It must have been father Blumhardt's special concern to acquaint his son with his own conception of the Bible. This Moettlingen was the son's spiritual home and nurturing soil. In 1852, when Blumhardt's witness "of what God wants to become in the world" had broken the bounds of church and parish, he was led to move to Bad Boll. Yet even when the son Blumhardt had to leave his parents' house to embark on further studies, it was Moettlingen to which he looked as his true home.

The study of theology, which he undertook more to please his father than from personal inclination, had no deep influence on him. As one who from earliest childhood on had witnessed a true history of God, he remained somewhat a stranger to the subjects on which his theology teachers lectured. He confessed that he "could not get anything out of theology or its negative and positive investigations in all their subjective diversity." Later, in one of his devotions, we find the significant words, "A God like that I could not believe in either. Already when I went to college I thought, if that is God, what you preach about, then I am through, then I don't want to become a parson. You have the same words, but you no longer have the thing. You set up a God without hands, without a mouth, without any feet, so that we can simply do as we like. God has to keep quiet and cannot do a thing. No thanks, I cannot believe in such a God."

Of course it makes a difference whether one grows up as a child in an atmosphere of God's nearness, or whether he stands in such a history of God as a grown-up man. The child somehow takes it all in as a matter of course. The man lives in it consciously and witnesses to it out of his own experience. Blumhardt suffered from being merely a kind of spectator of this history which took place before his own eyes. In those years he often felt miserable, especially seeing the abundance of true life which surrounded him. "I grew up, it is true, under the protection of my parents and of the spiritual fire which filled them at all times. Yet I felt excluded. Their life stood at a holy distance from me, inaccessible to my soul. Filled with a longing and a yearning, but unable to find anything that would enable me to take a real part in this life, I mostly went along my way in an inward sadness. Compared to the many who gathered around my parents in joyful, hopeful fervor, my own life appeared to me to be empty, indeed often almost hopeless."

Already at the time when Blumhardt was still officially vicar in the Church of Baden and Württemberg, he was on the point of giving up his pastorate. When his father called him to Boll as his helper, he only wanted to make himself useful around the house in the most modest ways. He performed the most menial tasks. "I thought only of helping my father in an outward way, even only as a cook." At times he actually washed bottles at the well and carried luggage for the guests; or he would wait quietly and humbly outside his father's door for any kind of job.

"But it was to turn out differently. Things which happened in my father's immediate surroundings gripped me in later years. My thirst for true life was quenched with one little drop of heavenly water, enough to awaken the same dynamic, powerful life which had gripped those earlier friends in Moettlingen." — "The light of something true, something real from God was shining from above" into his life. It kindled also in him the spiritual fire he had felt in his father from childhood on. It was then that a "little spark" entered his heart, giving him the living awareness that "God is! God comes! God is my God!" It was of this that he once said, "This little spark makes one clever enough. I can testify to it; I never learned a text nor could I ever remember a verse, but when this appeared to me I knew more within a week than all the theologians. Since then I also came to understand how the apostles preached." Now he was "God's pupil"; he was part of the "heavenly school where God himself is able to speak."

These events in his father's life which had such a decisive influence on Blumhardt refer especially to the death of Gottliebin Dittus on January 26, 1872. Her life story was interwoven with that of the father in a particularly holy and serious manner. Soon after her miraculous healing she moved completely into Blumhardt's house, where she became his indispensable helper. From this unusual and remarkable woman there went out a particularly deep sense of nobility, greatness and victorious faithfulness.

Her death became a turning point for the whole household. It drove everybody to repentance with a still greater and more decisive earnestness and gave the signal for a new spiritual impulse. This event especially influenced the life of the son Blumhardt. With it the true life which for him had remained at a holy distance until then, now broke into his existence. At the deathbed of Gottliebin Dittus he experienced the strange birth of which he later used to speak. He would hint at the significance this day had for him, saying, "That was my day, given into my heart. It was a night of death. We can still feel its darkness, and its brightness still shines for us. The open door that we have today is something which was fought for. It began with the death of Gottliebin. Her death opened up a new time for us."

Blumhardt even draws a parallel between the decisive hour in that night of dying, and what his father had experienced in Moettlingen at the sickbed of this same Gottliebin. "One thing alone caused the revolution in Moettlingen with the breaking in of Jesus Christ's great power of victory; the watchword then was 'Jesus is victor'. A higher battle was fought during that night. Again it ended with the cry, 'Jesus is victor!' For this we live to this very day. This one thing, the living contact with the Lord Jesus, remained. The Lord does not rest easy about the earth, about men. He goes forward step by step and allows His children on earth to feel the touch of His victory. In this way a forward movement of God's history becomes visible. This still stands and remains certain for us: Jesus is victor!"

Father Blumhardt also sensed what had happened in his son. No doubt this was what he meant when he wrote in a report about the last suffering and death of

Gottliebin, "From then on, recognizable to herself even in her dying, the new spirit broke in for all. This was the spirit she had longed for, for the sake of the Lord." From then on the son could truly be a helper to his father. Now he witnessed to something he himself had seen and experienced when he proclaimed the great truths which became revealed in the history of Moettlingen and Bad Boll.

The new life he had been given in his heart enabled him to be a support to his father when the latter's end suddenly and unexpectedly drew near and it seemed as though his death might bring into question his great expectations. The words spoken by the father in thinking of his death still betray a certain anxiety at first: "Since my time in Moettlingen I have thought a great deal about the nearness of the Lord. I witnessed a prelude, and if this were to disappear with me, think how hard this would be for me!" When he felt the true life in his son he overcame this anxiety and had new confidence. He continued to expect further manifestations of Jesus Christ's victorious power, also in the future history of Boll.

In this sense we may interpret the words of the dying man, as with a last effort he raised his hand and placed it on the son's head in blessing, "I bless you for the victory." — Joshua was a consolation to the dying Moses. He was to continue leading the people into the Promised Land, while Moses had to stay behind, weary unto death after the long wandering. In a similar way the dying father Blumhardt had a consolation in his son. In the trust and hope that the cause he had served all his life would be carried on, he blessed his son for the continuation of this task.

* * *

The death of father Blumhardt occurred on February 25, 1880. This was an extremely serious event for Bad Boll. All those who had recognized the significance of this place for God's cause may have asked themselves with some anxiety how it would go on.

From the first it was clear to the son Christoph that the marvellous history which had begun in Moettlingen and Boll must not be allowed simply to end with the death of its first bearer. For it was not the history of his father which they had experienced until that moment, but a history behind which Jesus himself stood with His victorious power. Christoph Blumhardt expressed this feeling straight away in the morning prayer meeting, after speaking of the father's last blessing: "Thus we feel that we have been blessed for the victory. Armed with this blessing we want to hold on firmly in patience and faith. We want to strive for the victory, so that all can clearly see what patience and faith can do. Praise and thanks be to God that even now we may place ourselves into the victory of Jesus Christ, who ultimately will bring salvation to the whole world." At the father's burial he said, "In the course of the years we witnessed marvellous manifestations of God in our midst. They all point us again and again to the fact that Jesus is victor. Our father is no longer with us; but we shall always have need of this victorious Savior. We must have Him and we shall have Him. From the grave of our dear father take with you the hope and the certainty that Jesus is victor!" As an expression of this sense of victory he started at this serious moment the old Moettlingen song, "Jesus is victorious king!"

Friedrich Zündel, too, spoke at the funeral service. He did not want simply to express thoughts of mourning, much as he felt the seriousness of this death. It was clear to him that even this event must serve the cause. To Bad Boll, the "dear Blumhardt home," he called out, "Continue in the blessing, the purpose and the work of your father! Your house stands and falls with the cause out of which it grew; for it is not your house, it is the Lord's. Hold on to what has been given you, dear house, that no one may steal your crown. The work of the Lord will go forward with you, for the Lord does not like to change or if you do not want to, without you."

At the end Zündel turned especially to Christoph, whose relationship to the father during the last ten years was so much like that of Joshua to Moses. At this unusual funeral service he read the words of the Lord to Joshua, "Moses, my servant, is dead; now therefore arise, go over this Jordan, you and all this people, into the land which I am giving to them. As I was with Moses, so I will be with you; I will not fail you or forsake you. Be strong and of good courage; for you shall cause this people to inherit the land which I swore to their fathers to give them. Be strong and of good courage; be not frightened, neither be dismayed; for the Lord your God is with you wherever you go." (Joshua 1: 2, 5, 6, 9)

This Joshua-like awareness, coupled with the whole responsibility of Joshua, became a determining factor in Blumhardt's life. He was filled with the awareness that the march begun under such powerful manifestations of God must not now lose its way in the desert. It must be led forward into the Promised Land. He felt the full weight of the responsibility placed on him for this continuation. True, he would sometimes say, "I do not deny that with my father's death something personal of God, which dwelled in him, has disappeared. Now we stand just about as he stood before his victory in Moettlingen." Yet he would immediately add, "But in the cause we are further ahead, for we have the benefit of his achievements."

It was characteristic of the time following the father's death, when he said in the morning devotion on Ascension Day 1880, "We must not think we are defeated now. Believe me, that hurts the majesty of Christ in heaven. We must not act as though the Savior were dead for us, weak and poor and lowly though we feel we are. The glorified Christ lives. He lives for us as He lived for the fathers. We shall yet experience that the more powerfully and courageously we uphold Jesus Christ's majesty, the more we will go forward. We must truly remain people of victory, for we have experienced something of the majesty of Jesus Christ. We know that it is He who lives, and with Him the faithful in this life and in the beyond. He lives, and the cause of the Lord must be carried forward victoriously! If only one little worm were thus standing firmly, all the world could not prevail against this one little worm!"

On the occasion of his father's birthday during this year of his death, Blumhardt said, "We are not dead, but alive. If something appeared withered and dying, I would be the saddest of you all. Yet I know that the Lord made us, and this is a source of joy. What He has made, He also sustains. What we have experienced is a new world. Truly, we already live in a newly created world. We live in a newly created time. This is the message of these days, and the time will come when all will see it."

At the end of the church year in this decisive period Blumhardt read in the *Daily Texts of the Moravian Brethren* the words, "Simeon waited for the comfort of Israel." On this occasion he spoke, thinking first of his father who was like a Simeon, and then continued, "Now we no longer have a Simeon. Now our house, as a congregation, must be this Simeon. We must stand as one man and represent this Simeon." When such a man dies, "one cannot simply say, this is the end. No, this man does not die, that is, if we carry on. Everything just goes on. Not even the thread is broken. It must simply go on in this same attitude of waiting. What has been given us through this waiting, to this day, must remain. Woe to us if we give up these fruits of our waiting in unbelief and drowsiness!"

On New Year's Eve, 1880, he said in the evening meeting, "We must not let the servants of God die, even if they have to leave us. They must continue to live in us. We must not think that now the cause has to decline because the founder of our life who achieved so much with his faith is no longer among us. Indeed, if we do not believe, then it will decline. But if we believe, then it will grow." During the first year after his father's death Blumhardt recognized and accepted his decisive task in this direction. It also determined his attitude in all the following years.

In fact, the father's death was not the end of the history of Moettlingen and Bad Boll. Blumhardt truly continued the activity at Boll, and in doing so he again and again experienced new manifestations of the Victor by whom that history had once been ushered in.

On the anniversary of his father's death in 1882 he said, "His death had to rouse us to new life. The Savior did not withdraw from us. With the father's passing none of what was most valuable for us in him passed away. Something divine protects us and leads us, and fills us with hope for ever increasing deeds of love from God for the world."

When other witnesses of the original history of Moettlingen passed away, especially Blumhardt's mother, in whom this godly life also pulsed with powerful originality, he said, "Now that upon which I had wanted to lean a little is gone. Well, I thank God that it is so. Now I want to see whether we stand on human feet or on divine feet. I believe that if we are true children, we shall just be carried. Especially when we suffer a great loss, when that is taken from us on which we actually wanted to depend, we feel strongly this being carried. This gives us joy; it comforts us. On the one hand we lose it; on the other hand we feel that we are being carried. Do not attach anything divine to a human being. If our cause were no higher than a human cause, I would not want to go on for another hour. But it does not depend on men. Therefore, do not give up! Do not give up anything of the most high, of that which is promised to us. Carry on!"

The true origin and nature of the history of Moettlingen and Boll is clearly shown in that it continued independently from the person of its first bearer. The fact that he was allowed to carry on his father's work was for Blumhardt a manifestation of this same victorious King who had shown himself so powerfully in his father's life. Years later Blumhardt expressed his joy about this in one of his Berlin sermons. "I am happy as a child that I, poor wretch that I am, was allowed to continue this work after my father died. For me to be able to carry on my father's work is the greatest miracle I can think of. All the circumstances seemed to be against it. This not my merit, for I was personally quite incapable of doing it. But one thing I did have: I thought, it cannot make any difference what I am when the Savior wants to step in." And some time later he wrote, "Is not the kingdom of God greater than the man who serves it? At that time God gave me the strength to carry on in joy and vigor as though nothing had changed, while everyone thought, this is the end of Moettlingen and Boll."

In fact nothing had changed. Just like his father, the son was a powerful witness of Christ's victorious power. His witness penetrated into ever growing circles, and out of ever renewed experiences the congregation at Boll was able to sing the old song of victory, "Jesus is Victorious King!"

* * *

Nevertheless, the history of Moettlingen and Boll was not simply to go on as before. Wherever divine history sets in through God's speaking and through the faith and obedience of His servants, it shows itself as history by the very fact that it does not stand still at something once achieved. It is carried on through new words of God, through new revelations of His will. Here Blumhardt showed himself to be a true servant of God. He was at all times open to such a speaking of God, and it led him on new paths. In part this was also the reason for the special significance which his life had alongside that of his father.

During the first years after his father's death Blumhardt gave his entire strength to the continuation of his father's work. Yet he resisted the fact that people would cling to the person of his father in melancholy recollections. They read too much into his name. In this way "one easily forgets what the Lord expects of us today and what He is concerned with now. . . . Therefore we should all strive to go on from the name of Blumhardt, in which the Savior blessed us, to that Name to which we are led: to the Name of **Jesus**. His strength and His Spirit alone can lead us on the way we are now expected to follow. The times change quickly. New tasks, new demands are made on us. Yet we also have abundant and ever renewed proofs of the Spirit and His strength. May the Lord Jesus strengthen us anew in His Name. May He make of us His servants in a pure spirit and give us alert hearts for the new things which will come."

This alertness to new tasks and new demands is characteristic of Blumhardt also in the time that follows. In contrast to the scholars and priests, who at all times are concerned only with "what is written" and care only to preserve what has come down from the past, Blumhardt was able to interpret the signs of his time. He understood in a truly prophetic manner "what the Lord demands of us today and what He is now concerned about." Basing himself on past words and deeds of God, Blumhardt was always attentive to the speaking and acting of God in his own time. At all times he remained alive to what God had in store for him. Thus there was in his life a continuity which permitted him to recognize and represent ever new truths.

The new things which came to him in this way never sprang from any kind of self-will; they were revealed to him in his listening and obedience to God's word. His life became in quite a real sense "like Biblical history." It brought into evidence truths of God's kingdom, truths that are of lasting significance for the church of Jesus Christ. Consequently Blumhardt was later able to testify, "The source of the living waters has revealed itself to us anew, with new recognitions and new demands." In his description of his father's personality we find the significant words, "His son, Christoph Blumhardt, continued the work in Bad Boll based on the principles of his father's life, and in part has drawn far-reaching consequences." Many such new recognitions and far-reaching consequences became visible in Blumhardt's life and at certain times characterized it.

One can rightly speak of different periods of his life, but never of mere episodes, surpassed and annulled by the following ones. In the history of God's kingdom on earth these truths do have their special times at which they manifest God's specific will for such times. They become visible in a decisive manner as the command of the hour. But they all belong to the one truth of God's kingdom. Thus it was also in Blumhardt's life. Blumhardt was fully right in saying of himself, in wonderment at the paths on which God led him forward, "I always went along the very same way. If anyone thinks I wavered or doubted, he is quite wrong. I merely went out of one shell, remaining the same inwardly, into another shell, only to break this last shell again and to enter another shell, so that I might be a messenger of the Gospel among all men." *

For years Blumhardt worked with visible blessing quite in the manner of his father. Then there came a time when, through several experiences, he felt certain that he should not continue his public speaking. His activity had led him into ever larger circles; he was causing a sensation on his mission journeys in Germany and Switzerland. At this very point he questioned his preaching activity more and more. His appearance in Berlin, where he preached in March 1888 more than twenty times and reached thousands with his word, was to be the climax and the conclusion of this activity. The great success he had obtained, outwardly seen, would have filled other men with satisfaction and gratification. Blumhardt, however, began to doubt the rightness of this way of representing the cause of Christ. Somehow he felt misunderstood by the masses who flocked to hear him. "I am terribly sorry that people say I am a famous preacher. May God grant that I again get away from all the fame men have given me. I don't want to be a speaker before you. I am no speaker at all nor do I want to be one. I want to be a man of experience. I do not merely want these things to be spoken about. I want to stand before you as a witness!"

After his return from Berlin, Blumhardt not only retired from his public preaching activity; to visitors

---

* The four volumes of Sermons, Devotions and Writings of Blumhardt correspond to the four main periods which I distinguish in his life and work. In each of these four periods Blumhardt's proclamation has its specific stamp, as the four titles try to indicate: *Jesus Is Victor! Die, and Jesus Will Live! You Men Are God's, God's Kingdom Comes.*

at Bad Boll it must have been even more striking that the healing of sickness, too, receded noticeably in Blumhardt's activity. He strongly opposed all those who saw the meaning of Moettlingen and Boll merely in these healings, and who sought only their health at Boll. He fought against Boll becoming an institution for faith healing. He greatly feared that the history of God which had become visible there might in the end only amount to the healing of sickness. "There is much sorrow in heaven because people want to draw the healing of their sickness into their religiousness; because they want to grab God's miracles for themselves. But my father certainly did not mean it in this way. And it is from him that they all have it. He did not want to draw down into the flesh the healing of sickness that was given through him."

In a special, printed circular letter to all those who approached him in their physical need and suffering, Blumhardt wrote these characteristic words, "In the attitude toward God, in a great part of prayer and religious service, there is a lie which turns everything in the direction of exploiting the mercy and grace of God in such a way that the Savior then becomes our servant. He is merely expected to restore again and again what we have spoiled. A selfish streak has crept in. This pains our hearts, and I decidedly wish to find a new attitude toward those who come to me in need and affliction.

"It is God's honor which we must now exalt in our own persons, both physically and spiritually. Not our own well-being must be in the foreground, but the one desire that God may come into His well-being, into His right on earth. His kingdom must gain ground in us and in our lives before we can enjoy all the goodness through the miracle-working hand of our Savior Jesus Christ. Now, many people write us letters just as they used to, asking for our intercession. We should actually answer in each case: Leave for a time your begging before God and first find the way together with us. Let us seek how we can do justice to God in the recognition of guilt and in the true striving for God's justice and His kingdom on earth. Turn your inner being to the opposite direction, and do not look at yourselves and all your suffering. Look at the suffering of God, whose kingdom has been held up for so long because of the lying spirit in men. Then be confident: God will surely not let you perish in your life, for you will be His true child, zealous for His honor."

For Blumhardt, even the conquest of sickness was justified only in connection with God's kingdom. As long as the kingdom of God and His justice cannot come to us, all our needs should point us toward this our deepest need. "There have to be signs of our deafness, our blindness, our dumbness! It must become clear that things are not right with mankind!"

Such was Blumhardt's new attitude to the healings which for many people had indeed been the essential thing in Boll. A deep-going transformation in Blumhardt's whole attitude came to expression. The true meaning of this profound change was indicated by him later on: "The acts of healing in Moettlingen were quite natural and understandable. But today we have gone further, and those who stop at that point do not even know where they are. At the beginning signs were needed. A trumpet of God had to sound; but it was not meant to sound for ever; it had to be silent later on. Other trumpets have become more important in the world. Not that it would not be a small thing for God to heal the sick; it happens more and more often, though very much in quiet. Yet it should not be proclaimed as though God's kingdom consisted in the healing of sick people. To be cleansed is more important than to be healed! To have a heart for God's cause, and not to be chained to the world, but to be able to move for the kingdom of God! This is the second trumpet-call to tear ourselves away from the traditional ways of Christianity."

This "tearing oneself away from the traditional ways of Christianity" is the purpose of that meaningful transformation in Blumhardt's life and work. He "became suspicious of ourselves, of our prayers, of our devotions, of our services of worship," in which he felt just that selfish streak. The enemy no longer attacked as the "dominion of darkness" against which his father had struggled and won decisive victories. No; the obstacle which above all stood in the way of God's kingdom was now "man himself, man in his flesh which struggles against the truth."

Therefore Blumhardt's fight now was directed against this flesh, and he sometimes changed the old song of fight and victory to say "Jesus is victorious

King, who also **conquers our flesh.**" By this "flesh" Blumhardt did not mean simply sensuality, but selfishness, and he saw this flesh especially where men behave in a very spiritual manner. He often spoke of the "Christian flesh" as the greatest menace to the Spirit of Jesus Christ. "If only we would all together and in the whole world stop worshipping our Christian qualities; if we would stop striving with frantic zeal to obtain the various pleasures they afford us; if instead we would all together sacrifice this to God in a feeling of poverty and weakness, and in the recognition that nothing is of any avail unless Jesus comes to life amongst us; then all our striving could very quickly become fruitful. But we have to make room for His life; we must die with our Christian flesh and fleshly works. In the spirit we can no longer seek such fleshly works nor spend ourselves in our zeal for them. We must seek God's kingdom and His justice."

Here the meaning of the new watchword, given to Blumhardt at this turning point of his life, becomes clear to us; it determined his whole message during this period of his work: **Die and Jesus will live!** With this watchword Blumhardt opposed all the selfish piety which only wants to have God's mercy for itself, and never thinks of making room for God's justice. "Justice, not mercy? No, justice! says the Savior; mercy can never be the share of the flesh. We must seek God's justice in our lives; only then can mercy come about. God is just when He allows our works to die so that His work may prosper. We should not be concerned with our pain and pleasure, but driven solely by the thought that once God may have pleasure on earth! The long outrage which we Christians have inflicted on Him must come to an end; then all creation will have joy in its God."

He severely chastised any "salvation-only" Christianity, that is, a Christianity so much concerned with its own salvation that it loses sight of the victory God promised for the whole world. "They hop around in raptures, crying, 'Oh, what bliss!' One is left completely speechless at the sight of these hopping, blissful people. They are happy, they are saved? Not I! While the world is teeming with sin and it is next to impossible for us to uphold God's kingdom, while God's name is being blasphemed and even good people no longer have any zeal for God, they are all in raptures? I would like very seriously to ask these Christian lazy-bones: What are you seeking? Yourselves or God? Your own cause or the cause of the Lord?"

With ardor and dedication Blumhardt turned toward the one great concern contained in the Lord's Prayer, "Thy name be honored! Thy kingdom come! Thy will be done on earth as in heaven!" He often closed his prayer with these three supplications.

Blumhardt also counted among those Christian works of the flesh the churches and confessions which demand for themselves a zeal and a dedication that is due only and exclusively to God. Father Blumhardt's move from Moettlingen to Boll meant in fact that he was leaving the church. The son was led still further on this way. "The year of the churches is past!" he used to say. He had in mind the church as well as all the "traditional ways of Christianity" when at one point he exclaimed, "All that has been until now is nothing! The old things are of no use! However you choose to understand it, soon we shall be saying, 'I count everything as loss, in order that I may gain Christ' (Philip. 3, 8). **Our** works must come to an end; only then can God create something pure from above. In our impurity nothing can endure!"

He could not understand the sureness of the church people, since he himself had deeply recognized how questionable all human religious structures are. "They are so stubborn as to go on and on in the same old ruts. Yet it is so easy to see that God wants to go different ways. This could even become disastrous, and no one should simply say, 'God is merciful again and again. He will maintain His church again and again.' Why, indeed! I would like to see the place in the Bible where permanency is promised to any human church. God does not care about the church if it no longer serves the cause. We have no guaranty that God's cause will be left forever in our hands."

Blumhardt also expressed his attitude toward the official church by stripping his own person and his whole house of all that had a "churchy" character. He took off his robe and gave the pulpit from the lecture hall in Bad Boll to a church in the Black Forest. At times he even desisted from giving regular sermons, nor did he make any further use of his right to celebrate baptism and the Lord's Supper in his house. A passionate revolt broke through in him, which did

AND HIS MESSAGE 53

not stop before any human sanctuary. "Zeal for thy house will consume me (John 2, 17). I no longer care for anyone, only for God!"

All this does not mean that his life was emptied of the divine spirit, but rather that his life was penetrated by it. From then on he no longer wanted to stand before his household as a pastor, but simply as a housefather among his family. All his talking became a witnessing to God; the daily common mealtime became the Lord's Supper; life as a whole became a service to God. All that was specifically of a religious nature receded into the background; but God's kingdom came to the fore and showed its full significance for the world in this new freedom from all religious and church limitations. Blumhardt freed himself completely from the pietistic manner and the churchlike forms of Christianity. He took very seriously the words of Jesus which determine this whole period, "Seek first His kingdom and His justice, and all these things shall be yours as well."

* * *

Uuder the banner, "Die, and Jesus will live!" Blumhardt tore himself away from traditional Christianity during those fighting years. This gave him the freedom he needed in order to understand the new way along which God was henceforth to lead him. He even exhorted the members of his household to strive for this freedom, and in the fall of 1896 he brought them the new motto which had been given to him: "Do become free human beings, and listen in freedom to the trumpet call of this day! Now it is important to hear the third trumpet. The trumpet which today resounds in the air says: 'Carry the love of God in your heart!' This will lead us further than all our Christianity. Today it is no use to sit in a pious meeting and make a pious face. Today we are told to go out into the world! Listen to the trumpet resounding in the world! This is true piety."

The "dying", the breaking away from the old ways of Christian piety, suggested that the divine was drawn into the world. This is meant in the deepest sense of the Gospel and its message of the heavenly kingdom which comes down to the earth, the Word become flesh. In this new period of his life Blumhardt is fully led into the world. He seeks the kingdom of God in the world, and not in any religious church-form; for the kingdom shall break in and triumph in the reality of this world. "Today one must be a man of God in the world. Those who do not understand this do not hear the voice of the Lord which has been clamoring for so long." — "Now it is no longer a matter of confessions and churches; those times are over. Certainly I do not want to be one who overthrows things, but in actual fact what is left is nothing but ruins."

The world-wide breadth and greatness of God's kingdom had opened up before him. "The kingdom of God is taking on colossal dimensions these days. We have come out of our little rooms, out of our isolation. The kingdom of God comes onto the streets, where the poorest live, the outcasts, the miserable. There the kingdom of God comes. It extends into the heavens and into hell, and to all peoples."

"The love of God is the key to the world." These are words Blumhardt wrote down in those days of the new beginning. They express what had gripped him so powerfully and henceforth was to determine his attitude to the world. In the period immediately preceding this time, the negative side of his fight against Christianity in its self-love, its smallness and narrowness, had been more in the foreground. Now, however, the positive meaning of the fight found its pure and powerful expression. The earlier fighting years remind one of a stormy day when strong winds sweep across the earth and lightning strikes down from threatening thunder-clouds. The new period is like a clear summer day when the golden sun lies quietly over the land and sheds its light over everything. It is the sun of God's love.

In this light Blumhardt saw the life and the love he was now called to proclaim and represent: " 'God so loved the world!' Whenever you feel something of God, you must sense that 'God so loved the world'." Here Blumhardt would emphasize, God loved the **world**; and if anyone were to ask, which one? the answer would be, "The world that became diabolical, the godless world." — "The people who lived in darkness saw a great light. The desperate, the condemned, the damned, the murdered, the miserable, those for whom there was no longer any consolation, no longer any hope, were allowed to see the Father. To them it is given to see the Father, who loves them. With every word of the Gospel, God lays a ban on the darkness, a loving ban, that is. God lays a ban on sin, death and hell through His love."

This love of God for the world was once revealed in the fact that He gave His only Son, and that in this Son He allowed the Word to become flesh. Christ in the flesh remains the pledge of God's love. Blumhardt, as a witness of Christ in the flesh, saw the whole world in God's hands. "Jesus is born, and therefore all creatures are loved." He proclaimed to all men, **"You men are of God!** Whether you are still godless or already devout, in judgment or in mercy, in salvation or in damnation, you belong to God! Whether you are dead or alive, whether you are just or unjust, whether you are in heaven or in hell, you belong to God!" "You man, listen: you are of God, no hell has any claim on you. The greatest sin is to degrade your personality, for I tell you, you belong to God." Joyfully Blumhardt confessed to this kind of "everybody's Christianity" for which his father had already been reproached. "Yes, I will gladly witness to it. This universal Christianity comes from my father's time, a Christianity that loves the whole world, that loves the sinners just as much as the righteous."

Blumhardt's attitude to the world and to man has nothing to do with the naively optimistic image of humanity which does not see man's true situation. Such optimism ignores man's fallen nature and does not take seriously the power of sin over man. It is true that man in all his weakness does have quite a lot of good things to show. Yet Blumhardt believes in man, not because of such virtues and merits, but because God believes in him and does not give him up even in his lost condition. "It is not because we love God, but because He loves us that we shall be saved."

With all its corruption Blumhardt still saw the world as God's creation; with all man's degeneration he saw him as God's child. If God loves the world, we may also carry this love of God in our hearts. If He sent His Christ into this human flesh, then we should not despair of man because of his sin. To fallen man in his sin Blumhardt proclaims the love of God: "Wherever there are sinners, there is the love of God." — "Jesus places Himself into the reality of sin, into the reality of our depravity, and not at all into the virtues which we may have. These he does not even see as real. To Jesus we are real because of our divine origin and in spite of our depravity." — "We need not despair about sin, for the Gospel tells us that Jesus was sent by God into the flesh, so that God's life in man may be rescued from the deception of sin and of death. Indeed, what we call sin and death is nothing but deception. True, eternally true, are man and God's creation."

Blumhardt saw the world with a heart full of God's love. Therefore he was allowed to see something in the world that was moving toward the kingdom of God; for "he who is of God sees life even in the world." It did not remain hidden to his eyes that in the world, where the pious see only godlessness and sin, there is a living spark of God's will to build up

His kingdom. Blumhardt took an innermost interest in world affairs and was alert to the signs of the times: "Since the year 1870 I have participated in every world event before God." Behind the human efforts to bring about a new national life, and in spite of their shortcomings, he saw that God's hand was at work. In contrast to the ways of theologians, who belittle and reject all that is human because it is relative, Blumhardt felt this relativity to be important for God's cause. "I am joyful, for something of that great hope which has become ours through the Christ of the world does want to come to fulfilment in our days."

This joy was due especially to the awakening of a new spirit of peace which made itself felt as a consequence of the first Peace Conference of The Hague. He attached great significance to any "international speaking of God." — "We may well take courage in our time, for we can see that the purpose of Jesus Christ goes through the nations. We experience much evidence of Christ's government for the honor of God."

He was all the more pained by the blindness and lack of understanding that believing circles in particular showed toward this working of God. "I beg you, do not mock! How many people will pray when the Peace Congress meets in January? I am very much hurt by our Christian newspapers; they have nothing but scorn for the Peace Manifesto of the Czar of Russia. Why are we Christians? For the sake of peace, people say. Peace comes from God alone. Men must pray for it, and if you do not pray for it, you are a devil. Mock if you will. You are mocking the Savior! Jesus said, Love your enemies; and when one of them comes in this love, people don't understand it. Therefore repent and believe in the Gospel! May God give us a fine, sensitive feeling for our time, so that we may notice the signs of the time!"

The striving for social justice was to Blumhardt the most significant sign of the times. He felt in it a "prophetic voice in the world." Underneath all the unrest and ferment of our time he felt the longing for God. Men took pains to improve their lives; they cried out passionately for a liberation from the pressure of their needs and demanded a new, more just order. In all this Blumhardt heard the call for the kingdom of God. "Now there is great confusion; now all the spirits are howling. It is a strange time. Yet even this is God's work. In quiet, God's cause is being prepared, be it through judgment or through grace. Finally people come into the kingdom of God; they know not how, the net falls over them." — "Today a storm is raging all over the world, for the world seeks a master. Even while she does not know it, she seeks her Christ. If the children of God do not cry out, then the stones must cry out. There must be a quivering and quaking, so that Jesus Christ can enter into the world at some point."

Just because Blumhardt's great concern was the kingdom of God, he had to approve of the cry for a new world in which man attains his right. However harsh, even godless, this cry might sound, there was in it nevertheless a more real truth of God than in all the religious and spiritual noise. "How can you be noble and religious, if you eat well and do not think of your fellow men who are starving? Today you have to think of them. It is a service to God when men stand up and say, 'I too want to live'. It is often these very ones, the so-called godless people, who toil and work in the vineyard. They are not 'churchy'. They pretend not to have any religion. Yet isn't it religion and praying when one strives for the vindication of man's rights?"

Blumhardt felt that basically the fight for a new social order was supported by a faith in God's kingdom promised us by Christ. The struggle for social justice actually became for him a sign of Jesus Christ. "We must not be silent. The social struggle of millions in our time is not a coincidence. It is related to the struggle of the apostles, and to the struggle which later also was fought by other men in secret, the struggle which we too want to fight. The ferment in the nations, the agitation of the poor, the crying out for the right to live — a crying, given into the mouths of even the most miserable of men, which can no longer be silenced — these are signs of our Lord Jesus Christ."

Blumhardt recognized the Messianic meaning of this social hope. He sensed in it something of the early Christian hope for a new heaven and a new earth where justice lives. Therefore he agreed with the Social Democrats especially in their complete rejection of the existing social order and in their demand for a fundamentally new world.

"The more ideal they imagine it, the more 'utopian,' as people say, and the more impossible it seems, all the more it will be said of them before God, 'They believe what Jesus wants!' They do not know that it is Jesus who wants it. They do not know that they now represent the thoughts of God, however imperfectly. Yet they do believe. They believe in humanity; they believe in a better regime; they believe in better conditions; they believe that one can become a person who is able to live with others."

More than once Blumhardt applied the parable of the two sons to the Social Democrats. "They are a tool of God, and are like the son who says, 'I will not obey my father,' yet afterwards does the father's will." — "They do not prattle about God; yet they act religiously." To the great annoyance of the nationalists they aspired to a new order also among the nations, with their International Workers' Associations. In Blumhardt's eyes this too had a significance before God. "The Social Democrats study for a reign of peace, they study theology; for peace is a part of God."

With all the "worldliness" of Democratic-Socialism, Blumhardt saw in it a divine truth. Not even its lack of church or religion could keep him from attributing to this general movement a great importance for the coming of God's kingdom. It also belongs to Blumhardt's prophetic nature that he saw God even in the godless and recognized God's work even where God appeared "incognito". This was incomprehensible and offensive to the pious who do not recognize such an "incognito". They would like to limit God and His working to the narrow sphere of their pious world. Blumhardt's appreciation of social justice shows the true Biblical spirit. It is the same spirit which once led Isaiah to see in the Assyrians the rod of God's anger, and which led the Second Isaiah to see a servant of God and an anointed of the Lord in Cyrus, King of Persia.

In the movement for social justice Blumhardt saw first of all a sign of the judgment. He heard in it a serious call to repentance for all Christianity. This movement wanted in its own way to reawaken the conscience of Christendom to forgotten truths of the Bible. "The social movement is like a fiery sign in the sky announcing the judgment. When Christian society sees itself confronted with a judgment, it should not be obstinate, but rather consider the truth that wants to come to it." This judgment which lies in the social movement not only means that our whole society is very much brought in question through the rising of the underprivileged and their demand for a new order. In a special way it is also a cry for a new, more just and humane order; a cry raised in conscious, often passionate opposition to church and religion. Is not the fact that the lowly and poor no longer expected anything of the church and of Christianity a terrible accusation against those who represented such a Christianity? They felt they had to wage their fight for a new world where man, not money, is in the center, also against the Christian religion. Does not this godlessness, for which the Democratic-Socialist workers' movement was again and again condemned by the believers, rather condemn those who have locked other men out of the kingdom of heaven by their manner of representing God's cause? Should not this godlessness much rather drive Christianity to repentance, than become a cause for self-righteous judgment?

The contempt and repudiation of the workers was directed against a Christianity which abandoned the cause of Christ to the powers of this world and cultivated a religion which all too often really proved to be an "opium of the people." If church and religion justify and protect this old world of money and force, of injustice and misery, while the unchurchly and godless strive for a new world of justice and of peace, of humaneness and brotherliness, then Christ may indeed "put all the pious with the devils and bring the godless into the kingdom of heaven," as Blumhardt once said sharply. Blumhardt sometimes spoke of a moral and working atheism in the world. He preferred this to a devoutness which does not understand the will of God in the world and opposes His command to go forward. Even in the French Revolution Blumhardt saw the hand of God. "If the angels will not do it, then God does it with devils." Now he saw God's hand in the social movement. He was therefore able to look upon all the commotions and upheavals, indeed the whole collapse, with confidence.

Blumhardt was not shocked by the materialism of which most Christians, from their lofty spiritual standpoint, accused Democratic-Socialism. He knew of the holy materialism in the Bible. As one deeply concerned for the kingdom of God on earth, he recognized the great justice which lay in that materialism. The redemption promised to men in Christ embraces their material life as well. The prayer for the daily bread for all men is also a prayer for the coming of God's kingdom, and has therefore found its place, and rightly so, in the Lord's Prayer. "Democratic-Socialism wants equal right to bread for everyone. It wants reordering of property in such a way that not money and possessions, but the life of men be given the highest meaning. Why should this be a reprehensible, revolutionary desire? I am certain that it is in keeping with the spirit of Christ to pursue such a goal. There will be revolutions until it has been achieved. It is no use to resist, for God wants all men to be equals in all respects. Even on earth He wants them to be not tormented but blessed creatures."

Blumhardt could speak in a very bitter way about those Christians who, for all their spirituality, have no understanding for this right to bread which is God's will; they see in the whole social question merely a question of the stomach for which they have nothing but contempt. "Our cause has become so spiritual that people have been drowned in spirit." — "How can we speak about spiritual goods in these days to people who look at us with eyes full of hunger and burdens? What use is it to prattle about the kingdom of heaven if you leave your fellow men in their fetters and bonds, the slaves in their chains, and the oppressed in their misery. You cannot even overcome the material differences around you because you are frightened of the poor and lowly. You just want to continue living in your hell! No one has any interest in such things these days. We live in the time of the proletariat. The poor are simply there, God bless them!"

Blumhardt saw in the social movement a sign of the times, a sign of our Lord Jesus Christ. He recognized in its goal a thought of God, and he himself belonged to these people. So in the end it was but a last consequence of this recognition when he went to the working people and held out his hand to them. Obedient to the voice of God which came to him from the social movement, he wanted to give expression to this voice and become the mouthpiece of the poor. "The Savior is with the poor, with the poor who have no voice. It is the Spirit of God which comes into the world of men, into the human world of misery, of suffering, of distress. There the Spirit of God sighs; it is as though this human world were forsaken by God. Jesus is in the hell which men make for themselves. The Savior goes first to the poor and miserable, passing over the pious. We too, in our religiousness, should feel drawn more to the lowly. We should bring them the Gospel, the joyful message that it will become better in the world. The sighing of the poor must have a voice. We have to recognize that the poor are justified in crying out for their human rights."

For the first time in the summer of 1899

Blumhardt participated in a large protest meeting. This meeting had been called in Göppingen after the publication of a bill for the limitation of the workers' right to coalition. He sensed the fear which this bill brought to the workers: "And where the fearful and suffering are, there one has always seen me also." To the great surprise of the meeting he himself spoke on that occasion and expressed his solidarity with those threatened by the bill, "I feel it is my duty to hold back no longer, to come forward and say publicly what I feel against this bill. It is a crime against justice!"

In the fall of the same year he spoke at a meeting which dealt with the employment of married women in factories: "I feel akin to these people who are reproached with pursuing utopian ideas. I feel I am on their side. I cannot help it, I have to say this. May the time come when it will be possible to give a new order to society, when money will no longer be the main thing, but the life of men."

On October 24, 1899, Blumhardt was especially invited to a meeting of the Social-Democratic Party in order to explain his point of view. In his talk he openly took a stand for Democratic Socialism. He tried to show the surprised and moved workers how it was just his Christian faith that led him to them; how he felt bound to them because of his religion. "Christ also proclaimed a new era. It was He, and not the Social Democrats, who first said, 'This world must be overthrown'; but Christianity has forgotten it. If what Christ taught 1900 years ago now suddenly wants to bear fruit in us, why should this alarm us? **Surely the Christian world order is not Christ's world order!** Believe me, I will stand with you with my whole heart, and I will work together with you for the new social order. We should, all of us, grasp the goal fully and completely and work towards it; this is right before God and men."

Sister Anna von Sprewitz, Blumhardt's faithful helper who had accompanied him to the meeting at Göppingen, tells of the impression which Blumhardt's words made on the masses. "I shall never forget the enthusiasm which followed these words. A little more and people would have raised him up on their arms." What a sensation his appearance caused everywhere can be seen by the fact that the news report in the Democratic paper *Hohenstaufen* was published as a special reprint in a pamphlet under the large heading, "Pastor Blumhardt's Avowal of Socialism." The newspaper *Basler Anzeiger* reported it in an editorial under the heading "An Act of Folly."

Blumhardt never understood this "avowal of socialism" in the sense of party politics. He was alarmed by this outward display which was made of it on the next day. But just because he had taken this step into the "world" in faith and obedience, he did not want to correct or revoke anything now. He willingly took upon himself all accusations of worldliness of which he was made a victim.

His own view of this decision is expressed in the words he addressed in those agitated days to his anxious friends who were unable to understand the meaning of his step: "My appearance in workers' circles, and in particular the support I lend to Democratic Socialism, has disquieted many. People have grown used to seeing socialism and godlessness as one and the same thing, and are concerned lest I desert my faith. The contrary is true. I believe, therefore I speak. Something of Christ lives in me. All my life I have believed in and striven for God's kingdom and His justice on earth. Now all this is expressed in this alliance of mine with the great workers' movement, with the poor who are fighting for their lives. Their fight is represented by social justice. It sets thousands of hearts afire everywhere. I see a sign of Christ in it; for Christ too wants a humanity which is wholly penetrated by justice and truth, by love and life. In the spirit I am united with this struggle. Let us not judge. Movements, even revolutions, have to be. Do not be afraid. Rather believe that our time, more than any other, is called to bring us closer to God's kingdom."

Elsewhere we find the significant words, "I pledge myself to the longing for a new era, not to a party. It is according to Christ's will alone that the world will be overthrown." By his decision Blumhardt was called to testify to the fact that God stood with the sighing and the wretched, with their hopes for a new world, and that He used them as tools for His goal.

Large circles banished Blumhardt because of his support of Democratic Socialism. Many of his former followers turned away from him in abhorrence. He had gone to those "godless people," just as Jesus once had kept company with the tax collectors and sinners. Now Blumhardt too, in indignation or in scorn, was called "a friend of tax collectors and sinners" (Mat. 11, 19). Immediately after the meeting at Göppingen the Royal Consistory asked him to renounce the rank and title of pastor of the Church of Württemberg. This goes to show the total blindness of the official church to the warning signs of judgment of this time, and to the word which God wanted to say to them through His servant. Blumhardt readily complied with this request. "State and church are no soil for the fire of God," he said in the prayer meeting the morning after he received the note from the Consistory.

There were those who could not understand why he did not take up the fight with the Consistory. He pointed out in a public declaration that his inward and outward development had led him already years ago to renounce the church privileges which had been given him for Bad Boll, and that it was now a relief for him to be freed of all obligations. He needed complete independence for his present activity, "an independence which cannot be given today to the servant of the official church, because the church no longer depends on Christ's commands alone, but on its own dogma and on state institutions."

Blumhardt was thus being excluded from the church and from the entire organized Christian world. The simple working folk, who were already alienated from the church, received him with all the greater openness and enthusiasm. In countless meetings all over the country he spoke to the people. They gathered everywhere in masses to hear his words in some overcrowded inn. On such occasions he was able to experience something of Christ's words to John, "And the poor have good news preached to them."

In all this it is especially important how he showed his new friends whence their social faith and their hope ultimately came. "The real depth and truth of the principles on which Democratic Socialism rests, can for the time being exist only where there is a certain influence coming from Jesus. In Jesus originates the thought and the truth that God is love. From Jesus comes this: man must also **be** love for his fellowmen. From Jesus comes the thought, the poor must have happiness; with the poor it must begin."

These people, who long ago had turned their backs on the church, who had perhaps exchanged their Christian dogma for an atheistic dogma, enthusiastically listened to him speak of Jesus. Now they were told of the Christ who wants to become Lord on earth in the new kingdom of God. Again and again Blumhardt experienced the reality of the parable of the great feast. He knew himself sent out as a servant onto the streets and alleys, the highways and hedges, to gather in the poor, and he also experienced how they came gladly to the feast.

For the sake of Blumhardt's witness through his association with the social movement, it would perhaps not have been necessary for him actually to step into politics. He was a-political. He believed in a kingdom and lived for a kingdom which is not of this world. In spite of this he allowed himself to be moved by the great trust of the people to accept a candidacy for the election to the legislative assembly of Württemberg, to which he then belonged for a term of six years (1900-1906). Some of his speeches in the meetings of the assembly may have been quite significant. He explained the absence of the five members of the Democratic Socialist faction from the swearing in by the King. He held a long speech against the grain tax, which would not really have helped agriculture but only raised the price of bread for the poor. He took active part in the discussion of new school legislation, turning especially sharply against the teaching of religion in schools.

Yet with all this one has the impression that Parliament was not the sphere in which his specific task could be developed. This time of political activity became for him an increasingly heavy burden, and in the course of the years he became more and more quiet. Even for his comrades he was obviously too broad and too great, too much a man, to be a true politician. They had once reproached him in this sense, and he had answered, "I am proud to stand before you as a man, and if politics cannot tolerate a human being, then let politics be damned!" At the end of the term he resigned from his mandate, and by making a journey to Palestine he avoided all efforts the party made to move him to accept a new candidacy.

* * *

Blumhardt became seriously ill on his return journey from Palestine. This illness was to keep him away from his household at Boll for a longer time. Blumhardt moved to Wieseneck, "the dear quiet home." From here he went over to Bad Boll, especially for the evening prayer meeting on Saturdays and for the sermon on Sundays. The seclusion and the quiet into which he withdrew from the agitated life of the last few years thus also found an outward expression. It gave a special imprint to this new and last period of his life and activity. Also inwardly Blumhardt kept apart from all the turmoil of the world and from all men's busyness. The new word which God had given to him was thus expressed in his whole attitude.

This new attitude was especially apparent in Blumhardt's position toward Democratic Socialism. Blumhardt had given up his parliamentary and other activities in the social movement. This could be explained by merely personal reasons, his shaken health, his age and the need to limit himself to the direction of Bad Boll. But there was more to it. He dropped the emphasis on the social movement almost completely from his message. He still followed the movement from his retirement with a real interest, and maintained the connection with the Social Democratic Party until his death.

Yet he did not expect anything decisive from its development and success. Blumhardt still spoke often about social justice in his personal conversations; but in his devotions and sermons he hardly mentioned it any more, in striking contrast to the preceding years. Even now he could sometimes say of the social movement that potentially it can "further the thoughts of Jesus in the life of the nations more than any other movement." — "In the social movement there lies an all-embracing concern for the pure human life; quite generally the concern that men be helped. This has been accepted by the broad ranks of the people and is an echo of God's will that all men be helped." He even added, "Christianity has never expressed so conclusively this principle, which lies in Jesus." At the same time, however, there is his verdict, "The social movement as we see it today still belongs to the world which will pass. It does not contain the fellowship of men as it will one day come through God's Spirit. Too strong a defense of prevailing opinions has a flavor which is disturbing to the pure service of God."

Blumhardt also criticized very severely the further development of the social movement: "The attempt to carry my idea of God into earthly things cannot take root at a time when men are filled with the hope that they and they alone can create a blissful humanity. Now they first have to run aground on the rock of earthly things, in order to grasp the higher things."

In reading such words one could almost say that Blumhardt was disappointed in the social movement. There may have been a disappointment in men, in their lack of understanding and readiness for God's call to them. However, this does not imply that Blumhardt had deceived himself about God's word for this time and about the answer God expects from men. By his stand for social justice Blumhardt witnessed to the word God spoke to our generation and to the truth that wanted to become reality amongst us. This witness retained its truth and validity even after Blumhardt was called back into the quiet from his task in the world. He had not joined the social movement prompted by a number of illusions, nor had he taken that step in an attitude of self-will or arbitrariness. He had done it in faith and obedience to God's word, which he had heard as a true servant of God. Such a witness remains independent from all personal satisfaction or disappointment and from all visible success or failure.

This witness with its whole meaning places our generation before a decision in the deepest sense. Our failure to act upon the clearly revealed will of God brings us ever closer to the judgment. In so far as the movement for social justice embraces the whole social problem and is not merely seen as a political movement trying to solve this problem, it implies even today the very question on which our fate will be decided. A terrible crisis now threatens to swallow us up; a crisis resulting from our lack of response to the social problem which knocks so urgently at the door of present-day society, and from the denial of the truth proclaimed by the social movement. It may well be, therefore, that the words "social movement" — as in fact all words we men devise to describe a way out of the need — are too small and inadequate to convey what this tremendous problem demands of us. However this may be, the truth to which this movement meant to point is today more burning than ever. Indeed, it is just this truth which stands in judgment over our time and world.

The full significance of Blumhardt's new attitude toward the social movement will become still clearer to us if we take into consideration that his attitude toward the church was a very similar one. This should be pointed out all the more emphatically as his indulgent tolerance was often interpreted as a drawing closer to the traditional ways of Christianity, once the object of his sharp attack.

Blumhardt did not expect a new community of men to grow out of a successful development of the social movement. Nor did he expect the victory of Christ's cause from the endeavors and undertakings of the churches. He called it childish tricks to try to achieve anything decisive through church reforms. He did not want to stake his faith "merely for a permanent church." He himself drew a parallel between Christianity and Democratic Socialism when he said, referring to the latter, "This human organization with its whole development and all the men who belong to it, cannot possibly represent the ideal. Whenever men with their nature seize on an ideal, something imperfect results, something harmful to the ideal itself. In the same way organized Christianity has not remained on the level of what Christ demands of us."

He saw the church as well as the social movement

in the light of the doubtful nature inherent in all human undertakings and movements. All this belongs to the world that will pass. Blumhardt's vision is directed entirely toward the world that is to come. For him all human organizations and institutions, be they of a worldly or a religious nature, receded before the one object of his entire faith and hope: the coming of Christ with His kingdom, His power and His glory.

Faith in the kingdom of God, the expectation of Christ's coming, was at all times Blumhardt's deepest concern. Like his father he opposed the powers of darkness and penetrated with a helping hand into the misery of sin and sickness, with the cry "Jesus is victor!" He opposed selfish and self-sufficient Christianity with the watchword "Die, and Jesus will live!" He entered into the world with the message of God's love, associating himself with those who believed in a new kingdom and fought for a new humanity within the world. At all times it was the faith in God's kingdom which determined his attitude.

However, his activity was not to exhaust itself in the healing of the sick, which at one time appeared to many as the main meaning of the history of Moettlingen and Bad Boll. Nor could he persist in his fight against traditional Christianity. He had to renounce his activity in the social movement; for it could never bring forth anything final or perfect in the growth of God's kingdom on earth, though it was significant as a judgement and a promise. The fundamental purpose of his life and of his entire active witness and fight was to show itself in all its purity toward the end of his life. Far above all those material forms it pointed to their deepest meaning and to their final fulfilment.

Thus Blumhardt stood in this time and world like a faithful Simeon waiting for the promised comfort of Israel. No unrest, no wrongness, no corruption of this world could make him waver in his expectation; he lived his life within the promise. In the midst of the existence and events of this world he already lived in the promised future of Jesus Christ. He was able to wait patiently in this world without succumbing to it. He did not surrender any part of God's promise for what was still to come on earth. "I wish we could live completely in the promise; for the promise is something substantial from God himself. Again and again it renews our strength, our hope and our experience."

In the parable of the begging widow, Jesus lays it on the hearts of His disciples to pray without ceasing. Blumhardt, who preached repeatedly about this parable, really prayed at all times and did not become lax in his prayer. As one truly chosen he called day and night to God for salvation from the enemy. All human concerns receded in him before the one main concern: Thy kingdom come! — "We want to be a people which for the sake of the misery in the world is able to say always and first of all, Thy kingdom come!"

Blumhardt knew that in this waiting for the kingdom of God there lies a strength. "Waiting is a great strength. Waiting is a great deed." This waiting is not inactivity, not a passive attitude; it is but the strongest expression of the fact that man expects the decisive power and help from Christ and His coming kingdom. In a true waiting attitude, however, man may prepare a way for this coming of God's kingdom. Through his waiting he even becomes a co-worker with Christ. "Let us arise in the knowledge that a Christian is a helper in this hope, full of the strength of waiting." — "Truly waiting people, true Christians who wait for the day of God's mercy upon all men, may gently spin the thread and twine it around the nations, tying them to our faith and preserving them for the day of Jesus Christ. What a coming of Christ that would be if many Christians were to say, 'I too want to do something, I want to be a strength in quiet, through my waiting for the sake of the others.' "

This very waiting for God's kingdom frees man from the powers of this world, from the trust in its strength and from the fear of its forces. In this freedom he is able to recognize God's will, to take up his task, to do his work, to fight his battle, to take his sacrifice upon himself.

To the true waiting for the Lord also belongs the hastening toward His future. The waiting soul knows that the Lord is coming and goes to meet the future. The waiting soul is directed toward the working of the living God, and allows itself to be led by this working. The waiting soul understands that which wants to come into being in history according to God's will, and gives its strength to this growth. All this may, through

God's power and help, become a service to what is to come.

Thus man's true readiness for what God wants to do in us becomes an inner preparation for God's working. Man's efforts in the tasks willed by God for the hour becomes a cooperation in the work which God is doing among men in order to lead them toward His day. "Watch for my future! the Savior calls to us. If we fulfil this task, if we watch for His future, it will be as though His future were coming into our present time. Again and again new life is given, new developments, something that opens up the way along which we can go. Each time it is a piece of Jesus Christ's future. Christ's future is not one single point in an absolute remoteness for which we are to wait. This hardly thinkable; we would probably all go to sleep over it. The future is already present."

Therefore Blumhardt not only speaks of a future coming of Christ, but he prefers to say that the Savior is on the way. "The Savior is coming. He is not quietly sitting somewhere in eternity, waiting for a certain moment when He will suddenly plunge in. He is on the way. We may at all times have the future before our eyes. We may expect it each day. The coming of the Savior runs through Christian history, through God's working in the world, like a thread. If this thread is not to break, the Lord Jesus must ever be coming. There will be new ways. New revelations will enable us to continue working and waiting. There will come a time when our watching and waiting, which at all times has prepared the coming of the Lord Jesus, will be consummated."

So firmly did Blumhardt stand in this expectation of Christ's coming that his constant prayer, "Lord, Jesus, come!" often gave way to the certain promise, "The Savior is on the way." His great and main concern, "Thy kingdom come!" again and again became the joyful message, "God's kingdom is at hand!" Thus Blumhardt knew himself called to be the doorkeeper: "I am only a doorkeeper, nothing else." He saw his task simply in standing by the door to watch for the coming of the Lord, and to keep the church of Jesus Christ constantly alive in this expectation through his call, "He is on the way!"

Blumhardt's whole attitude was determined by his waiting for the coming of Christ and His kingdom. Therefore his retirement from the world could never mean giving up the world. The Christ he expected comes as the Lord of the world. His kingdom is the kingdom that has been promised us for this earth. Even now Blumhardt looked upon mankind in faith and hope. He no longer stood as a fighter in the midst of the world, but rather as a priest apart from the world. He carried this world on his praying heart and constantly interceded for it in a priestly manner. "Our blessing must support all that men do, so that the splendor of God may penetrate all of men's striving." — "By our prayers we help in the new creation."

It was Blumhardt's special concern to gather a church that was to stand with him in the future of

Jesus Christ, and to prepare the way for the Lord in living expectation of His coming. He expected little from the church as an organization of Christianity. Yet he felt the existence of a **living church** of Jesus Christ to be of decisive importance. He visualized a church, placed in the midst of this world, that looks toward the coming of God's kingdom; a church that holds fast to the truths of the coming kingdom even against the kingdoms of this world.

To his friends who gathered around him he said, "All your love and attachment to Bad Boll is worth nothing. Unless you want to stand with me in Christ's future, you will still be separated from me." In his eyes the only value and significance of Boll lay in the fact that here people were led toward the coming of the Lord. It was a place where they lived in the growing of God's kingdom. "The character of our house is the expectation of God's kingdom. Whoever enters the house will feel that here people want to stand quite directly in the growth of God's kingdom and participate in its coming. If he does not feel this, he understands nothing of Boll."

Blumhardt was filled with the need and importance of such a place for God's history among men. "God always wants to have a place, a community, which belongs to Him really and truly, so that God's being can dwell there. God needs such a place from where He can work for the rest of the world. There must be a place on the earth from where the sun of God's kingdom shines forth." We may well say that Boll was such a place, far beyond any human understanding or perception. However, not only in Bad Boll and around the person of Blumhardt was there to be such a community. "There must never be a Bad Boll Christianity; God protect us from this."

On the contrary, it was Blumhardt's special concern that such a waiting church-community should grow, apart from this place and independently from his person. A Zion of God, a people of the promise in whose midst God can begin his work, should arise from all the nations, out of all the churches. "A people of faith is needed upon whom God can lean and to whom He can give the victory." — "There must be a people who carry this faith and this hope in their hearts. Men partake in their own creation. Everything stands still, unless there are men who make an effort to become God's helpers."

Blumhardt wanted to invite everybody to join this people of God. Even the simplest human life becomes significant when it understands this call, "You little human being, the Savior needs you. It is not at all a matter of indifference; you also belong to it. See to it that you are filled with joy, with love, with delight for God's kingdom. He needs such people; and in His future, the only future we have, He needs you." It is to this living church of Jesus Christ, not just to any human church, that the promise applies that even the gates of hell will not prevail against it. This living church may be only a little flock in our world, even in our so-called Christian world. Yet it is to this little flock that God wants to give the kingdom.

The living church of Jesus Christ has the special vocation to uphold the light of the promise amidst the darkness of the world. When all the spirits and powers of this world are unleashed and would seem to cast a doubt upon this "growth of God's kingdom," this is just when the church-community has a special task. It is therefore very significant that during the World War (I) such a community was given at Boll. In those years world history showed its true face in unheard-of horrors and destroyed all human hopes for a happy course of human history. Yet Boll was a place where even now, and now more than ever, people lived in the expectation of God's kingdom. Even in the darkest hours they clung to the faith and witnessed to the rulership of the Lord. The promise of the kingdom was the firm ground on which Blumhardt stood through all the tempests of the time. While the lands were filled with war and battlecries, here was a "Zion of God" where the peace of God was preserved in the hearts of a few on behalf of the whole world. While the nations were drawn into the curse of the powers of this world, here was a man who carried in his heart the faith in God's kingdom and the expectation of His final victory.

By this faith and expectation beyond all human bounds, Blumhardt give to those around him a firm leading in the midst of the general confusion. In the midst of all discouragement they found through him new strength for the cause of Christ. Blumhardt had always expected, in connection with the coming of the Lord, a revelation of "sinful man". Therefore, when all the antigodly and satanic powers in the world revealed themselves, it could not make him waver in his faith and in his hope. Indeed, it was clear to him that God would reveal His will in just such world events. Even such times of judgment would ultimately have to serve His cause. "Human history seems always to be without God. Yet God's will and working run through everything. Ultimately His will is done."

Shortly before the beginning of the war Blumhardt said, "We are threatened by a catastrophe and everybody speaks of war. This can lead to a shaking up in many hearts and open up something in them. The time will come when God himself speaks and Jesus Christ, the Lord, is King on the earth. Therefore we must remain firm, however great and manifold the evil in the world may become. Today we stand in a crisis, in a judgment. It is a kind of end which we expect; for the present must cease and make room for the future." At the end of this sermon he prayed, "Let us remain firm in the promise. Let us remain faithful, even in stormy times. Strengthen our hearts, lest we fall into doubt, however great the disaster may be that befalls the earth. Thy rule remains great and strong in eternity. Finally the time will come for which we are waiting, when thou wilt reveal thyself in all thy glory."

In this attitude Blumhardt experienced the outbreak of the war. In this attitude he remained throughout the war. The waves of enthusiasm for the war carried everything else along with them. The representatives of the church even undertook to place God at the service of the nation. Yet Blumhardt stood high above the din of war and remained firmly convinced that finally God would make the nations and their doings serviceable to His cause. In one of his very first wartime sermons he emphasized that in human history a higher will rules than the will of men. "The first thing we see, born of the wilful 'I' of men, is fighting and quarrel, anger and war and bloodshed. Our world is a world of sin, and all sin comes from the self-will of men and of the nations. But against this there stands another 'I': 'I will pierce your fear and sadness, your sins and your crimes, with my peace!' In our time human will brought us the war; the human way of thinking, I want to be greater than the other one. And yet the 'I' of God, the will of God, remains greater than such self-will. Be comforted: Through all this pain, through all sadness, world history leads toward a great peace. This is the end for which we wait. A hopeful future lies before us. All sadness shall find a hopeful end."

The very fact that now all the evil in humanity was revealed, was in Blumhardt's eyes an occurrence which must serve truth. "All the evil that lies in humanity must be revealed somehow and come to the surface. If men hate each other in times of peace, very well, then one day you will have war because of your hatred. If one wants to become greater than the other, then this must also become quite obvious at times. In this revelation of sin, of evil, of foolishness, of crime, there lies a progress. So let us put up with it and be quite alert to all that we experience. Let us remain firm in the hope that this history has to belong to God's kingdom. It has to lead to the goal, to the end of sin, to the ultimate great peace which shall come to the earth according to the promise, Peace on Earth."

He prayed, "We can believe that in the midst of a terrible world thy kingdom, O God, will be planted, that thy kingdom will grow. Lord God, Father, have mercy on men! Have mercy on their times, their generations and nations! Have mercy within all boundaries everywhere on the earth! Let the light and the power of thy kingdom arise in the dead and death-bringing humanity!"

Blumhardt saw the war as a judgment which had to come over the nations. God is at work in the judgment. Therefore good must finally come out of it, "for God's judgments are never only to our hurt; the end is always good." People have to understand this meaning of war; they must repent under such a judgment. "The most important thing in this war is not the sum of events, the battles and murdering of countless human beings, but what lies behind it all. It is a sign of God, a language of God, and we are to learn from it. Our time cries out to us all, Repent! We all have a guilt in this war. All the nations have helped to bring about the final outbreak. We must all together repent of what is happening today. Therefore do not sleep, but awaken! Watch and pray! The kingdom of heaven wants to come near."

Blumhardt remained free of all hatred against the enemies. In his eyes hatred is the real enemy against which the fight must be waged: "The real enemy, Satan, the enemy of God and of men, is the deathly hatred against other men that wants to invade our hearts." Therefore he warned those around him, "We are not only Germans, we are citizens of the world. We must be able to pray also for our enemies. We must be able to love all men. Mankind belongs to God in Jesus Christ." — "We must let our hearts be moved by the misery of those whom we call our enemies. They are not God's enemies. Englishmen, Frenchmen, Russians, Germans— they are all one: they all belong to God." Nor could Blumhardt rejoice over the German victories. While people were in a veritable frenzy of triumph he said, "You rejoice over the victories, over battles won. I feel a shudder going through the whole of nature when I hear people shouting, 'We are victorious, thousands of the enemy are killed!' We cannot rejoice over this, my friends, we cannot!"

In these times of war Blumhardt longed for a different fight and a different victory from those of the battlefields. At the beginning of the war he prayed, "Let this fight be turned into a fight for thy heavenly kingdom, for the salvation of the world. The victory must come after long afflictions!" He remained certain that finally Jesus would arise from this fight as the victor. However many afflictions there may come, one thing is for ever certain: Jesus remains the Lord. All things must expect His victory, and in His victory everything must be swallowed up. He will triumph! This war is merely an occasion for Jesus Christ to reveal himself as the victor. Thou, God, canst not let the history of men go out of thy hands. We believe that Jesus is the victor. He remains our trust, our salvation and comfort." For this victory of Jesus Christ, His living church is of decisive importance. Jesus needs people who in the midst of the chaos of world history fight His battle. "We must quietly stand by the one and greatest lord, Jesus Christ. Take your place in the ranks of those who fight for God's kingdom!"

On the first Christmas in wartime, Blumhardt called his household to this fight, "And still we must hold high the banner, we of God's kingdom; the banner of our Savior Jesus Christ. He wants to bring in the day. Even if it should take a long time, we have Christ's day in our hearts and do not let it go. It is our calling to preserve Christ's day in our time, in the midst of all the horrors of our time. In this we want to remain firm and never give up. The coming of peace will depend upon those who have Christ's day in their hearts."

Blumhardt recognized the power of Satan in the war; but he faced this evil with the weapon of light: "Jesus, the light of the world, will come!" He led the battle against the powers of darkness which his father had once begun. Again and again in this fight he sang the old song of Boll, Jesus is victorious King! The faith in the victorious King, "who, with His might, from the darkness leads to radiant light," became for him the only strength to prevail in this fight. "My only strength is to wait for the future of

Jesus Christ." — "Everything, even our time, is now aimed at the future of Jesus Christ. We must not lose sight of this, lest our sadness become so heavy that we can no longer bear it." — "We live in a dark time. It is a time of death, a time of earthly powers and not of the heavenly kingdom. The kingdom seems as though lost. But now arise, you people of God; and you, man of God, arise! In the midst of world's night we are to have a light in our hearts. This light is the hope in our almighty God who gives us help in all our ills. Our present task is a quiet, trusting expectation. Be people who wait for God! Be firm and look only toward the goal which the kingdom of God will bring to us!"

To the last Blumhardt remained in this quiet, trusting expectation. He detached himself more and more from the dark today and already lived in the bright tomorrow. "All of world history must be pushed away from us. We must put away everything. In this serious and important time a people must be gathered who really eat and drink only in God's kingdom." On New Year's Eve, 1916, this attitude of his was again expressed in a significant way. "Come what may, in joy or in pain, in war and in peace, at all times we can walk in heaven. In great things and in small things we remain steadfast in God's will on earth. In this way we can overcome even the hardest times; we can endure. Faith and hope, that is our task; and to wait for the Savior, our Lord Jesus Christ." In a simple, yet powerful way this also came to expression at his last evening meeting on September

29, 1917. To the Bible text (Isaiah 49, 7-13) he only added these few words, "This is the promise. It will at all times remain a light on the earth. We may walk in this light of the promise. Often it appears to us as though God had forgotten us. Yet He remains with us. His word is living and true, and we may be comforted. All things will yet come into His hands!"

A radiant light lay over the last years of this man of God. Like the dying Moses on Mount Nebo, after all the battles he looked calmly and confidently towards the Promised Land. At the same time a childlikeness radiated from him that shows us clearly the truth of Jesus' words, "Unless you turn around and become like children, you will never enter the kingdom of heaven." (Mt. 18, 3)

Blumhardt gave us an image of himself when he said in one of his last sermons, "He who looks into the eyes of children looks into the heavens. We too are still children. The childlike qualities which God gave us at our birth must triumph over the darkness and keep us joyful in good and in bad days. Unless we believe in a childlike way, unless we trust as children do, in all circumstances, and remain joyfully in our childlikeness before God, we are not worthy of the kingdom of heaven. The kingdom of heaven does not want great men; it wants a child. The greatest are those who remain childlike, even when they become great and famous men."

This childlikeness showed itself in an especially moving way when, soon after his last sermon, on September 30, 1917, Blumhardt suffered his first stroke.

In this sermon he spoke of the Sabbath, saying, "In Jesus Christ we have Sabbath every day." At the end he prayed, "In our sadness let there be works of the Sabbath, for thine is the kingdom and the power and the glory and also the peace, which will come for the praise of thy name." Sister Anna recalls, " 'Now the evening of rest has come,' he said almost joyfully after this stroke, and from now on he waited for the hour of his homeward voyage like a happy child waiting for Christmas Day." Of his last waiting she says, "He was extremely touching in his helplessness, always filled with joy and gratitude like a happy child. His intense prayer life was very moving. Often he lay quite still with folded hands or whispering softly, yes, come, Lord Jesus! Amen. Then a blissful expression transfigured his features. In the last days of July 1919 one felt that the end was near, and in the night of August 2 he passed away very quietly and peacefully. He lay there like a happily slumbering child with the expression of victory."

There were hard wanderings and battles in store for the people of Israel, after their great leader left them. However, behind them there still stood the man of God who had led them through the desert, and who had parted from them with a firm direction toward the Promised Land. We too are in the midst of that dark night of the world, the beginning of which Blumhardt experienced. Indeed, we feel more and more clearly that the hardest part of the end time which he expected is yet to come. Yet we too are supported by the promise that had been entrusted to this man of

God; he had set it up again among us. In the midst of confusion and darkness, while the whole world is going to pieces, we are able to find our way and to remain upright only through the faith in God's kingdom and the hope for its ultimate coming. This faith and this hope were newly opened up for us by Blumhardt.

The powers of corruption which at present inundate all things shall not remain victorious. Faith alone can give us the certainty that Jesus Christ stands at the end of the history of men. World war, world crisis, world need, and all the developments which press on toward new, still more terrible catastrophies, all these reveal to us the end toward which our world history is driving. Yet Christ stands behind this end. Therefore we may expect it in the light of His promise, "Behold, I make all things new!" The light of this promise alone can illumine the darkness which lies upon our world. Thus we learn particularly in these times to understand more deeply what God wanted to say and give to us through this powerful witness of His promise.

Blumhardt's fight, his message of the truth of God, become all the more significant today. The words written over his grave shall henceforth witness to this truth, which he will represent among us also in days to come:

CHRIST'S VICTORY REMAINS FOR EVER SURE. THE WHOLE WORLD WILL BE HIS!

R. LeJeune

Talks and Sermons

1

CHRIST THE LORD

The Lord has risen indeed.   —Luke 24, 34.*

The crucified one, who is now the risen one, is the Lord. This we must believe. We have not gained much if we take it for granted that Christ died and rose again. Many people assume this and yet go into the path of hell. This assumption is of no use to me unless I make Jesus my Lord. The fact that many people cannot believe that Christ rose from the dead is not the worst yet. At least they see it as a tremendous thing, too tremendous to believe. The sad thing is that some claim to believe it and yet are not concerned with it and do not make Him their Lord.

When we hear about the resurrection of Jesus Christ it should shake us to the bones. "What? Somebody has risen from the dead? Who is it? That can't be! The whole world has to change if this is true!" Anyone who is not struck in this way has no idea what it means to be crucified and then to rise again. This must sink so deeply into our hearts that we gain a new attitude to life. It must strike us so powerfully that we make this risen one our Lord and accept Him as the Lord of the world. We must acknowledge that all things belong to Jesus. Why? Because He has risen from the dead. Therefore all knees must bend before Him and all tongues must

---

* Bible quotations are taken from the Revised Standard Version unless otherwise noted.

confess that Jesus Christ is the Lord. There cannot be any creature either in heaven or under the earth which is anything beside Him. For this we live and strive.

The only real Christians are those who under the impression of the resurrection of Jesus Christ lay claim to the whole world in the name of the risen one. For they alone know that it will be only a short time before Jesus Christ becomes the ruler. He who merely assumes that Christ died and rose again is no Christian. He is simply a man with certain opinions.

A Christian, then, a warrior and fighter, is one who concludes from the resurrection of Jesus Christ that the world will now come under the rulership of God. He knows that as a Christian he must help toward this goal. We, as the living church of Christ, must live in constant struggle towards the great rulership of the King, Jesus Christ. This makes us Christians.

2
THE POWER OF GOD

>Because the poor are exploited, because the needy groan, I will now arise, says the Lord, I will help. —Psalm 12, 5

How? How will God do it? That is always a puzzle. Everywhere in the Bible you can read, "Go away, let me do it!" Sometimes it certainly sounds as though God were complaining that He could not yet manage it. Yet then comes a time when He says, "I can do it after all. The needy and miserable are before me; they need my help." But how will He do it?

Much can be said to answer this question. The faint-hearted say, "Oh yes, He is able to bless me even in my misery, and after all there is eternity." But in this way not a single need is overcome, not a single tear is dried. This business of eternity — honestly speaking, I have certain misgivings when people always comfort me with eternity. If I don't see any help in the world, who can guarantee me help in eternity? Or has the Savior come only into eternity? I think He has come to us! Therefore this comfort is not sufficient. It is true that in many temporal situations the goals can be found not within our earthly life, but beyond it. The question remains, however, whether the goal is reached immediately after I leave this earthly life. That I don't believe; God's history in the world isn't so mechanical as that. Things happen more spontaneously and the fight is more difficult than we think. We cannot just dance around in this world and then die and assume that everything will be all right in all eternity. No; developments take place here and now. There are advances or retreats, depending on how much of the misery can be taken from us and how far God is able to help us.

It lies within the power of our God to make us happy. He has to use power; we have to believe in it. This is what God created us for. If there are people who in their spirit serve this power of God, these people will draw into our world a little of this power and will thus become the best representatives of God. It is not so much the question whether a man suddenly decides to be converted. The first and most important thing is that God sets out to intervene for him and in the end wins him. The history of our redemption moves forward in times when God's help is shown in deeds which we have done nothing to bring about. When the day comes that we are in the kingdom of heaven and when the last jolt has come, we will be surprised, if we look back once more, at how much God had to intervene for us. Even against our will He had to use His power to save us. God, who is in heaven, comes to meet us. He forces His way more and more toward us until He breaks through into this world.

This is God's intention in His efforts for us. Help will be delayed, and misery will not be overcome, until the barriers between eternity and this world are broken through. A hole must be made from above downwards, not from beneath upwards. Christendom sees it just the other way round. Christians see nothing but holes upward to get away from the world; they want to fly away like doves and be saved. But according to the Bible the holes must be broken through from above downwards, in order that help can fly down to our earth. At present it costs a terrific fight for that to happen again. Do you know why? Because nobody believes it. They all want to get away and be saved, and they don't even know what is beyond. They even hurry to die; but when they get there they rub their eyes. It hurts me that Christians generally don't understand this. That is why things go from bad to worse.

I know well that people will say, "Here comes old Blumhardt again with his queer stories." But please prove to me which of the two is according to the Bible, our death or God's future for us. From the first to the last chapter, the Bible deals with the coming of God into this world, and nothing is said of this business of dying. Each word in the Bible guarantees to me deeds of God right where I stand. God needs but to lift one finger against our misery, and more is achieved than if we founded a hundred welfare institutions. This is how we have to see it. Something coming from God also has to happen in the near future; for we can't force it. We must ask God to intervene; we have to become Biblical. This is all I want to say: become Biblical again! Understanding and wisdom will be given if our first concern is that God come down and that Jesus come down. We should lay claim upon our earth-right, the right to the victory over sin and death here on earth, not by our faith but by the power of God.

Our own poor and weak faith is of no avail. Most people believe according to their own ideas. It sounds harsh, but I can't help it. I can't stand it if people always babble about faith; it makes them terribly egocentric and they rely only on themselves. I also know what faith is; but the kind of faith we ourselves make, where we wish to force something according to our own ideas — that is not what I want. I say it is the power of God which redeems us and which will surely redeem many people, even those who do not really quite believe. Who can stand up and say of his faith,

"Look, I have the true faith." That is an illusion! Once we go back to the Biblical reality, a light will penetrate all our actions. Our hearts and minds, our hands and feet, will be completely changed if we bear in mind God's efforts to enter into our world and to achieve something here. It is not sufficient just to have a religion. The heathens too have a religion; it isn't enough just to have one a little bit different from theirs. God doesn't care about our religion. In times when He could not come down to help, He preferred to let the people become irreligious. In Egypt the Israelites could do whatever they liked and they went to rack and ruin. Yet He sent His help to them; for His help does not depend on men's religion, but upon God's faithfulness and mercy and power. It depends on hearts that wait for Him to come down.

Let us be united in this hope and certainty that God sees the miserable on this earth and then says, "Now I will rise up. Now I will give help." And we know that the great help will be given on the day of Jesus Christ.

3
GOD'S ALLIES

> O Lord, hear; O Lord, forgive; O Lord, give heed and act; delay not, for thy own sake, O my God, because thy city and thy people are called by thy name. —Daniel 9: 19

Thus prayed Daniel, and not without result. One can feel this from the whole prayer. He is praying about important matters. He is praying for the liberation of his people from Babylonian captivity. One might have said, "This is God's affair. He has brought trouble on us; He will raise us up again if He wills it. It has been promised that it will happen one day. We cannot do it." Daniel did not think this way, however, but rather, "Since it has been promised, I will make it my cause and I will not rest until it happens!"

He is quite right. God can expect of him, and of all who believe in the promise, that they will put their energy into doing God's will on earth. For in a certain sense God takes us as His allies. He is glad to have us. This is because the earth is, after all, in our hands. Man has a very great weight in the destiny of the earth. Men can either withhold the earthly things from God, or they can give them to Him. In our earthly life we can live for God's honor or we can live as His enemies. This globe is like a small kingdom, and its prince is man. If things on earth are to run according to God's will, and not according to Satan's, then man must be God's ally. God cannot set up His kingdom among us unless we do our part. In fact, one might say that even for the smallest thing that God wants to do on earth He looks for a man and asks him, "May I? Shall I? Do you want it also?" And then He does it.

Certainly He could do it differently. It would be a small matter for Him to take our position from us and say, "You stupid people, why should I bother about you? Go away. I am the ruler!" But we, as His vassals, are not to be removed from this position, but shall be respected in our vassalage in spite of our sin. God upholds the position which was given to man in the beginning. Man shall have the earth; God holds him to this. Everything that God does is done through man. One day it will be revealed how much grief has come about because man has not exercised the rulership to which he was appointed by God. As God's ally he has not brought God into his earthly life. Then God will say, "Why have you not let me in? I would gladly have helped you, but you did not seek me. You have not called on my power. With great enthusiasm you let yourselves be taken in by other powers. When I offer myself, you do nothing but yawn; it just bores you. But when spiritualism or some other kind of panacea appears on the scene, you are all in it body and soul."

And so it turns out eventually that man has made his own misery. Our greatest suffering is caused by the will of man, who in his independence has fallen in with false allies. Man has to become God's ally; he has to throw his whole being into this alliance. Then he will be able to rule the world up to the clouds and down into the depths and upon the earth.

The whole trouble is that there are so few who grasp this. Daniel was one of them. And God is kind. If there is but one who prays rightly amongst the many, God accepts it as the prayer of all. He thinks, "The others are too stupid, they do not know what it is all about. If they knew, they would pray like that, too." Thus it is possible for one with a generous heart to intercede for the many. And now the Lord Jesus is here, who with an all-embracing heart intercedes for us all. Following Him, the living church of Jesus Christ should intercede for all. We are the chosen, the priestly people who are to represent the others.

What is the purpose of our existence? To make sure that we are speedily saved is not the main thing. Anyone who thinks that is making a big mistake. The most important thing is to be fighters and to bring the world under God's feet. The main thing is that we should be the voice of justice on earth and no longer tolerate the rule of sin and Satan. Then we are allied with God. In this struggle we shall triumph. We Christians together are now allowed to be like Daniel.

Christ's cause stands still unless His church is alive. God has patience even up to this day; just as Peter says, "It is not God who hinders the cause." The future of Christ, the coming great redemption, is not delayed by God. God is not responsible for the tedious history of the church. He is patient and says, "I am waiting until you come. I will not interfere too quickly, in order not to spoil you. That is why it goes slowly. But if you hold out as my allies, things can move forward."

Thus we are now called to be allies of God. I am not a Christian so as to seek my own salvation in an egotistical, self-loving way. I am a Christian for God's sake. I am a servant of God, who fights for the cause of Jesus Christ.

The earth lies before us like a great estate that has been weather-worn and laid waste, and whose ancient title deeds have been forgotten. The living church of Jesus Christ must take God's interest to heart and study these documents to find out what is to be achieved by this fight. Now if we take up an alliance with God, we, as representatives of Christ, may read these title deeds of the earth, and there we shall see that we have been terribly injured. We shall find that the evidence is in our favor. Now it is a matter of starting a lawsuit against the devil! Through sheer deceit we have been tricked out of our rightful place, and now it is a matter of restoring rights.

Our first step is to go to the highest judge, that is, to God, and say, "God, have mercy on us. It cannot go on like this. We have fallen into the adversary's hands. Help us!" Then God answers, "I do see your misery, but it is your own fault, not mine, because you have lived this way. Yet I am just, and it is also to my interest to see that you regain your rights. So I will help you." In this way the proceedings begin that shall help us to win, and we shall win. In studying the deeds we shall find out that much has already been fought for successfully by the intercession of Jesus, and we could become very active in striving to assert the rulership of the living church on earth; for this is newly guaranteed by the person of Jesus. The verdict has been given, but it has not yet been carried out in reality.

Now the living church of Jesus Christ should give itself heart and soul to carrying out the judgment which has already been spoken on the enemies of mankind, on sin, death and the devil. Then God's victory can truly come, and man will be set free according to God's will.

Let this be our concern. In this way we would not only become a Daniel; we would also know what God has promised, what our right is. We could take a stand and say, "This is what we want! It has been promised us by the almighty God; it has been guaranteed us anew through His love." It will come in the end; in the end there will be a people who cry, "Lord, hear us; Lord, be merciful; O Lord, give heed and act! And let us wait no longer! But for thy own sake, my God, delay not; for thy city and thy people are called by thy name, and according to thy name it must be that thou shalt at last rule on earth."

4

BEHOLD, I MAKE ALL THINGS NEW!

> And he who sat upon the throne said, Behold, I make all things new. Also he said, Write this, for these words are trustworthy and true.
> — Revelation 21, 5

This word of God, "Behold, I make all things new," shall accompany us on our way out of the year **1886.**

It shall not be in vain that His voice was heard on earth. When God himself steps forward with His "I" so that people on earth can hear His voice, He places himself in the temporal. Even though at first there is only one who hears it, through this one many of us and finally the whole world will hear it. While everything perishes and escapes like a stream, and threatens to drown in the flood, the Almighty stands on the heights. When He speaks a word, feeble man can grasp the Almighty by this word. Then flee, ye years! Perish, thou earth! We no longer belong to you. We hold in our hands the rope by which we swing ourselves up into heaven, from where we heard the voice.

Even in our day we are allowed to hear this voice. Let us this evening open our hearts to the grace of our Lord Jesus Christ, that we may all hear the voice of the Almighty who made heaven and earth. Therefore it is to Jesus that we give our whole hearts tonight in gratitude, in love and in trust. He makes the almighty God known to us, so that we may partake in the throne of God for our life, which truly needs a throne, a government. One glance at our wretchedness makes us sigh for a firm support which will never pass. This firm support is Jesus Christ, who has come near, who has come into our flesh. We can feel Him, grasp Him, take Him into our hearts as our brother, in order that we may have the support of the almighty God in this world. If you are willing to go from one year into the next in this way, all is well for you; then things may run as they will, the earth may turn as it will, our trust is in the throne of God.

But I would like to ask you very seriously: Have you become aware that the almighty God offers himself to us in the Lord Jesus now, independently of the times and independently of circumstances — that because of this we may enter into His kingdom, which is everlasting, and step out of the earthly things which perish? Here much is lacking still, my friends, especially with the Christians. It almost looks as though the Bible were of no use to us, since so few of us completely grasp what **God in Christ** means, what it means that you are in God through Christ and no longer in the world through your own self.

On this evening we can make no better decision than to take refuge in this word of God and to ask God that He may protect and keep us in it. There are many words of God, and we all know them. We need not go far to look for them; for since our youth we have been taught how to understand the living God through them. But the greatest word which crowns all the others is still this one, "I make all things new!" This word very particularly lends itself to being a support and a comfort if we become aware of how fleeting our life is and how quickly everything passes away and becomes dust and ashes. **All things new!** This is God who cannot tolerate what is corrupt and destructive but wants to repair it. Into this comfort of the living God we are allowed to enter and want **to enter now.**

Of course we enter into this comfort only through repentance. Many people do not consider sufficiently all that must become new. They think of all sorts of things around them and often not at all of themselves. If they do think of themselves, they would like to have only certain things changed so as to be able to carry on more comfortably. They never consider that all things must become new, everything within you, around you, everything in the wole world, all things in the whole of creation. We should be deeply humiliated to realize that there actually is nothing which must not also become new. If I were to take a close look at each one of you — all of you must become new! It is all wrong! Your cause is worthless!

However, there should be something of which we could say, "Now this does not have to become new, because it already is new!" Do we not have Jesus Christ, who rose from the dead, through whose grace we can be born anew? Of course we have Him, but frankly speaking it almost looks as though we did not have Him. Whatever one experiences of men, one still has the impression that there is a lot that has yet to be renewed. Even where something has begun, it is often tangled up with men's own, old nature. So even if something new may appear to be there, one feels like saying, "Oh, away! Away! Away! Everything must become new!"

This is how things are, my friends. A darkness has come over Christianity in regard to this very matter of renewal. We are so easily contented and so quickly satisfied with a Christianity that makes us a little more decent. That is all people want. And yet if one takes a look at it one must say, "This cannot be all." No, my friends, what we have cannot yet be all. All things, all things new! Not just a little taste of something new, but **all things** new, in yourselves first of all. Oh, that we all might feel the longing for something new to be given again. How long have we been sitting around here; how long are we being preached to; how long have we been receiving impressions; how long have we let ourselves be admonished again and again! And still there is no break-through to something new. What are we in our villages, in our towns, in our families, in our own hearts? Things just will not become new.

This could depress us very much. Instead, it should unite us in repentance. Repentance means turning with our whole hearts to the word in which the living God pledges himself. We should call on this God and say, "Yes, dear Father in heaven, in our Lord Jesus it shall become new, all things shall become new. But you see, nothing happens. Why do people not turn around? Why do they not receive strength against sin? Why can they not come out of their evil, out of the devil's cunning and power and temptation? Why is it that nothing happens? And even if a little does happen here and there, even if at times you work a sign among us and heal someone or free someone from the devil, why doesn't it become new? O Lord our God, this really is a terrible misery; nothing becomes new with us! Have mercy on us, O Jesus Christ, our Savior!"

This should be our cry, my friends. I say this to you in my house as well. Or do you think we are the ones? There are so many proud people; yet they have nothing to be proud of. They are intoxicated by their Christian piety, and each one thinks in his mind that he is the one, that he's got it. But I have never yet seen that anyone was born anew. You are still the same as you were ten and twenty and thirty years ago. You aren't new yet! And we must become **new,** else our house will stand on the earth which passes away, and our cause will be lost. It is a question of life or death which has to be decided urgently: **either all things become new, or everything simply stops.**

This is true for each one of us. Unless you are renewed you will perish, and you might as well join in the stream of death together with the whole world. But as a Christian, my friends, as a disciple of Jesus, one should be horrified to have to swim along in this stream of death. Defend yourselves, then! Overnight Satan comes along and takes hold of one after the other. Then, in your misery, you will lie in the dust, and what will you do then? Unless you are renewed you will perish like everybody else. Oh, that I could open your eyes, that you might help me cry out! Then you would see that we are bound, that we are in chains. Then you would see that all customs and practices are arranged in such a way that every person trudges along at the old monotonous pace, till finally he is laid in the grave. People throw earth over him and go back home and continue living just as dully and superficially as before. People are not in the least different from what they were fifty years ago. They remain just the same and don't really want to be turned around.

Therefore, my friends, turn to God! What did Israel do in the ancient times, when the tabernacle was gone? They also let things drift foolishly for a long time. Yet several then rose up and cried out, "O Lord our God, renew us! Let your glory come over us anew. We want to be your people, we want to be a fellowship in you, in the Holy Spirit. Let this renewal be, Lord our God, for we are afraid. If it does not happen soon, what is to become of us?"

"Behold, I make all things new!" He says it — we want to believe it. But in order to believe, we have to repent; without repentance you had better leave it alone. If your eyes are open to what is lacking, then believe! He does say these words, and we want to lean on them with our whole spirit and carry them in our hearts, however bad things may look now. He does not say, "Perhaps, if possible, under certain circumstances, I will make things new, but I have to think it over." He says straight out, "I make all things new. It will work out somehow, even if much patience is needed. I will certainly do it." So again and again we have reason to think that He will do it. Especially if we give ourselves, then one day a beginning will be made with us.

This promise belongs to our time as well as to the future and to the past. It is ever ready in heaven to renew anyone who wants to become new, who is ready to give up his possessions, who does not push his own person into the foreground and does not love his own life. For such a one the word in heaven is ever ready to bring about a renewal.

Therefore let us believe that the one or the other of you will be renewed. Just try it! Go completely into repentance and then fully into faith. It can yet happen; I do not give up hope. Even if but a few became new, it would still be something. And finally all things shall be **made new.**

Even in facing the judgments which have come over us and which may yet come over us, we can lean upon this promise in faith. You know very well how things are amongst the nations. The murder weapons are ready. The powers of darkness have risen and want to drive things to the point where the earth becomes a pool of blood. Satan knows quite well that if such a thing came about, it would be the end of the preaching of the gospel. Then the Lord Jesus might as well leave. Then people will be thinking of war and all spirits will be overpowered by it.

So we are faced with a grave matter. Do we want to let it slide? I should say not. Help to hold it up! Think in faith of the words, "I make all things new!" Must there be war forever? If that were so, then He does not make all things new; then I don't believe it. If we cannot pray for the time to come when God's almighty arm will hold up warring armies, then it is not true that God makes all things new. Yet it is true that He makes all things new, and therefore I believe that there is something we can do to stop such things from happening.

But of course if everything is to be made new, then something must break in, not coming from us but from heaven. A new deed of God must happen; something living and real from the Lord Jesus must break into the physical world. It must become visible that Jesus really lives, that the almighty God really is, and that He will not let himself be pushed to one side for ever. It costs a hard fight, my friends, until finally something becomes new; for people just don't believe that God does something from above. They do say, "He guides the destinies of the nations"; but then they call everything God, even when it is the Devil who does it. Yet no man will believe that the almighty God really intervenes. A lot would already be new with us if only we could think: He will really, personally intervene in our physical world; the time must come when we shall be able to pray that such threatening dangers may be averted, and our prayer will be answered.

There are still other things which threaten us. Even if war does not break out, there will still be a hailstorm of disaster over the whole world; only you will not see it all in a mass. Last year millions of people lost their lives all over the world through all manner of trials: tempests, landslides, explosions below and above the earth, earthquakes, epidemics, all kinds of accidents which are to be expected in the hectic life of our days. At the same time there is an enormous amount of sickness of body and soul. How much sighing there is in hospitals, how much misery in the mental homes. How many people are pining away with the most horrible diseases. How many are being killed, some slowly, through envy, through hatred, through the maliciousness of people towards each other. If all the people murdered during one year were gathered up, they would make a large pile. One doesn't even need guns; they perish anyway.

Every family must be prepared for something to happen suddenly that will disturb their peace. Then we have to believe and pray that the judgments may be turned away, and that something new may be given to you and yours and to the whole world, indeed to the whole creation, something from the heavens above. If God keeps His word, my friends, then we can stand up against anything, especially if we ourselves are already living in what is new. You should sometimes place yourselves in what is new. Try it! God often tries to see whether He can do something with this one or that one; but they don't quite grasp it yet, they remain lame. Arise and go to meet what is new! Pray for it. Something new must begin, coming from heaven to strengthen our trust that the whole world will yet be renewed through the almighty power of God.

This is what Jesus Christ wants. For this reason He is the first-born from the dead. He does not want this tedium to continue forever; He wants to have things new! For this Christ was born; for this He died and arose; for this He is sitting at God's right hand. Go to meet this renewal, so that it may come!

This is what we must believe; this is how we must see what is new. What, then, is new? What does "new" mean? New means what Jesus is, what is in heaven, what God is. It means what is as old as eternity. Strictly speaking, we in our sin are "new." Sin is not the oldest thing; it came in as something new. God is the old one, the eternal one, who was from the beginning and remains in all eternity. We are just ordinary upstarts. Therefore, the new thing is what is old, what is in heaven, what is eternal, what has no beginning and no end — God himself. The earth must be transformed into something divine. What is earthly must become eternal, what is temporal must be re-created and turned into something primarily divine. Just think, my friends, what it would be like if things could begin a little to become really divine; if even the physical would no longer be wrong, but would be transformed into the divine. How happy we would then be!

To be sure, when the divine comes about, then look out: Then one cannot just drag along one's own wrongness. Then we shall pass through a judgment, through a fire. Then we shall have to be purified, to become gold, not wood. Then we must give up everything, give up what is false. We must become completely **true,** just as what is in heaven is true, just as the Lord Jesus is whole and true and all the angels are true, and God himself.

So you also must become true. This is what **new** means. It is comforting that this new thing is not something unheard-of. It is at our doorstep; it is already on the earth, and it is not at all unheard-of. I have already seen something new. Whoever has had a little to do with the Savior sees something new, and therefore I can well imagine that things will become new on earth. Yet however much I may preach about it, people still don't see the heavenly things in Jesus Christ. So much was new already in the apostles. So many new powers came with the outpouring of the Holy Spirit, where the natural had to yield to the new, the heavenly, the eternal. It could make one die of grief to see how little has actually happened. So much that is new lies before us, and still there are no results; it is always at our doorstep, and still it will not come in.

Perhaps, my friends, once you know that to become new means to become heavenly as Jesus is heavenly, you will also understand that it can come easily as soon as we become alive in the Lord Jesus. The gates of heaven are quickly opened, especially if we gather in greater numbers to call upon God. Then the devil will surely be afraid. For he knows that the heavenly things are the old, the original things, and that our sin and our death are new things, wrong things, which have come into the world but don't belong in it at all. And if we are faithful, then the heavenly things will belong to us; God and Christ will be ours. All else is the devil's and is none of our business.

Now you know it, my friends. Now you can grasp it in faith and in repentance, so that you may reach out for the heavenly things. Love the Savior! Believe in God! Seek His word and keep it! Be zealous, be faithful! Jesus Christ is our brother. He hears us at the right hand of the almighty God and can quickly answer. Oh, that it may come to pass in the New Year!

5

WHEN GOD HID HIS FACE

I said in my prosperity, I shall never be moved. [But when] thou didst hide thy face, I was dismayed. —Psalm 30, 6-7.

Such verses should always remind one of historical events. They are not just the kind of religious feelings we have, but quite solid events, as for instance with Moses. When the people of Israel went out of Egypt and suddenly the waters drew back and all the people crossed to the other side and were safe, they thought, "Now we shall never be moved; never again shall we succumb." And when they saw the Shekinah,* when they saw how manna fell from heaven and everything was put in order under the direct guidance of God, the people felt extremely exalted. But then, when the people had sinned and God hid His face, and they no longer received an answer — then "I was dismayed!"

We can hardly imagine these things. In the first place we have no idea how one can talk with a Shekinah. Nobody in the world knows anything about this. We have no idea either how it is when God is angry, for we don't notice the difference. We see much misery, suffering, need and misfortune, even in our Christian affairs. Yet everything is so confused that as a rule we no longer know what is God and what is devil.

Only with a very sharp vision can we expect to have any discernment. Certain uniformities of feeling come about in which we drag along. But that is not the real thing. The real thing is the clear perception, "Now the Lord is here!" or, "Now something is wrong! Oh dear, what has happened?" For instance,

---

* *Shekinah* means habitation of God, the light of God's majesty which reveals His presence among men.

when Achan had stolen — how gay the people had been before! — suddenly things stopped. "What is going on? What is it?" The slightest blow was like being killed. The thought that this was the end, that the thread that bound men to God had broken off, made their world crumble. So it was then; it was something tremendous and we can no longer imagine it.

It is no wonder that today many do not believe that there was a direct relationship with God, not just now and then but lasting for centuries. The prophets said again and again, "The word of God was precious in the land." This does not mean that there was no Bible; but people did not attach so much importance to the Bible, for they were used to being guided directly by men of God. They thought: The Bible is of no use to us unless we have prophets. And if there were no prophets for a long time, they were dismayed — then God was remote.

Now suppose we also have something like that, and it breaks off; then we also are dismayed. It is a pity that in our days there is so little dismay over the fact that divine things come to an end; when they do, we just carry on in our earthly ways. Here and there one may be appalled by a misfortune that befalls someone. There is no such thing any more, though, as being dismayed as a people when the divine power is not there, when — symbolically speaking — the tabernacle is lost. And still I wish that this dismay would come back.

I would like to transport our Christians with a

jolt into the emotions of early Christianity and then back again with a jolt into our present-day emotions; with a jolt to the side of the Risen One who speaks at certain times, and into the fellowship of the Holy Spirit who speaks at certain times. Then, looking again at our time, we see nothing but human chatter. Always and in all things it is man, man, man! And God is silent. I am not satisfied with the ways of certain Christians who say, "The Lord has spoken with me. The Lord has said to me thus and so." If only it were true! The thoughts one makes up in one's head, even if one means it quite honestly, are far from being the Lord. Yet the very people about whom one knows for certain that the Lord does not speak with them, are surest of all about it. Where one knows for sure that something is not from God, they claim with greatest assurance that they have it all from the Lord. They do have inspirations of spirits. There are demons who chatter with the piety of angels. They are so pious I can't keep up with them! But when human opinions want to represent what is divine, and when that which is truly of God has to withdraw shyly into the background because the human thoughts make so much noise, then things become difficult. Everything becomes lame and poor, and countless hungry and thirsty souls are neither fed nor watered. All things run in a lower religious sphere. There is no divine clarity. If light is again to come, man must again be silent and God must speak.

Will the light come? I hope so; for a little of it is here, but it is hidden. A fine thread runs on, which is not of men. So also in Israel for a long time a brooklet ran silently along, and finally John came, and then Jesus, and then it began anew. Now we are in the same position. It also began with a Shekinah; the Holy Spirit of the new covenant is none other than the voice of Jehovah of the old covenant. Yet then it disappeared underground, and now all is quiet, just as in the post-Babylonian times. We too should now feel dismayed, because on the whole we are stuck in the world; we don't find the way out and upward into the light. Therefore we should pray, "Lord our God, do not let us shuffle along in this way any longer! We have studied more than enough, and we still don't accomplish anything new. Therefore arise and **speak** again! Speak down from heaven above, speak now to the whole world!" For in the end thy glory must break in over the whole world!

6

THE LAMPSTAND OF GOD'S PEOPLE

The Lord will judge His people and will be merciful to His servants. —Psalm 135:14

We want to be God's people everywhere, in all places. The Savior shall work on us in the power of the Almighty; He shall not leave us unattended. This is how I should like to interpret the word "judge." The only danger to which we are exposed is that God might say, "You can go! I don't care about you. You can do as you like." That is the worst thing that can happen to anyone. The result is that someone in heaven comes and blows out the lamp. The light is out! Or, if an individual is concerned, someone comes with a pen and crosses out his name. Then it is like the words in Revelation, "I shall spit you out of my mouth." That is, you are never again mentioned in heaven.

We do not want to be amongst these. We want to belong to those who are mentioned in heaven, who even may be allowed to gather as a people whose lamp is lit in heaven. This is my great wish. There does not yet exist a full and equal representation of us all in heaven, on the basis of a wholehearted, united striving for the kingdom of God. The lamp has been blown out and it will cost a great deal of trouble to get it lit again. True, there are little lights burning, where there is true fellowship in the Lord Jesus; of this we may be certain. Yet we do not have a lampstand in the real sense of a living church. For when that is there, then things will really start rolling in the world, then things will no longer be so monotonous. However, we should not underestimate the fact that at least some individual men have a little light up there; for things on earth do keep going, though in distress. My longing, however, is that a living church may come into being; that many may live in peace and unity, because they have the same light in heaven, however diverse they may be on earth. That is our longing here at Boll.

I know that I expect a great deal of my friends; do not believe that I find it easy to say things that others don't say; it is one of the heaviest burdens I bear. Yet I cannot be silent; it must be said again and again, and I repeat it today: There is no living church, no people whose lampstand burns in heaven. There is so much godlessness on the earth, because God is not there in the way He should be. Otherwise the godlessness would be restrained through His living church. Often it seems as if God were saying, "Let them go. It doesn't make any difference what they do now. The confusion is already there." So there is no restraint or governing. Yet nothing is more dangerous than a people without rulership. Therefore our hearts should be filled with the entreaty, "Savior, rule us again!"

Certainly, then we must stop being obstinate; for when the Savior rules, things happen in a wonderful way. It may be, then, that we must let go of what is dearest to us, of what we have in the past held as most precious. We must be flexible. A man who is waiting and praying for the kingdom of God has to be capable of changing. He must be like a servant who always watches the hands of his master, and never knows what the next hour may bring. He simply holds himself ready. In this way we shall become a people who are allowed to serve, who experience powers and signs. Above all we shall experience God's judgment. We shall experience His infinite mercy, just because everything is under the judgment. Then judgment and mercy are woven together in a living way, and God can do great deeds; then we shall say, "Jesus lives! Not I have done this, but Jesus Christ."

Such a people of Christ should gradually be gathered. I mean it as it says in the Bible: out of all peoples and languages and tongues. Therefore let me say, too, please don't be so terribly German, so terribly French, or Russian! Don't be surprised if God's people come together from all kinds of nations. When once the Savior starts working, then things will not go according to our boundaries, nor according to church boundaries. All kinds of blossoms will grow up out of the ground, which can no longer be brought into any ready-made pattern. Therefore we must not bind our persons to anything except to Jesus. Therefore anyone who wants to belong to the people of God for the fulfilment of God's kingdom, must always be ready to act, ready for Jesus' word of command, so that human slavery can never find its way in. In saying this I also think of my own household. To anyone who wants to take sides in the name of Boll, one must say "No." Only he who enters into the fellowship of Jesus in a clear, simple way, and makes His loving influence felt on all sides, belongs to the true people of God. Then powers and signs can be given.

If only this could soon become clear, and the lampstand of God's people were burning again! Then many things will be put in order again. Then things need not be worked out behind the pulpit; the true laws of Christ will again be enforced. Then the mighty shall be brought low and the small, the genuine, shall find its true value. Things will again be according to Christ instead of according to the world. Nowadays the clever dominate and the foolish are treated as second class people. In that day the miserable will be comforted, the troubled will be eased, those who are bound will be released, the blind will see, the deaf will hear, the lame will walk. Every time we see a blind or a deaf man, a sword should go through our soul. Why? Why do the blind not see, the deaf not hear, when the gospel includes this express proof of genuineness: "The blind see, the lame walk, the deaf hear, yes — the dead rise." Why? Why?!

Therefore our prayer to God can be: Light our lampstand! Then I shall no longer be afraid. The things that cause us so much grief will be gone at once. The terrible confusions of the soul, the temptations and bewilderments will stop, for our lampstand is lit! And our angel, the messenger between us and God, is once more on the way. The connections are made again. Things are working again on earth, after the stiffness—centuries long—of the members of Christ.

7

A NEW FOUNDATION

This poor man cried, and the Lord heard him, and saved him out of all his troubles.
—Psalm 34, 6

It is not always quite so easy as many think for God to save people from troubles. They believe that God need only move one finger and they would be helped. This is quite true. Yet God cannot always move His finger. He could, if heaven had come to earth and God were able to say, "Now the earth is my place and my house, where I can live and freely rule as in heaven!" As yet, however, the earth and especially our human life on earth is in many respects not at all under His rulership. Many people do as they want and use their freedom to destroy God's will.

Naturally, therefore, God cannot simply save us from earthly troubles, for this would often be directed against himself and destroy His own essence. So if we want help in earthly troubles, we should not start to cry here where our need is, but must reach out to the great need of the world. We must first seek the **kingdom of God,** in the small and individual things as well as in the great and general things. First of all the soil must be prepared. A **foundation** must be laid, even in the tiniest things, if help is to come. We should observe this down into the smallest details, and not just pray superficially, "Help me with my headache or with my fever!" We should first of all ask, "How close can the kingdom of God come to me? Is there a foundation so that I can simply say, 'Free me from my headache'?" There has to be a justification for this.

Now there are people in whom there is no justification whatsoever. It is quite wrong to think that merely because one is a Christian he has the right to expect God's intervention for himself. So people protest against God and say, "Why? Why does not God help me, why is He so cruel?" But there are people, and even nice people, who are completely under the power of the fleshly life. They themselves and their surroundings serve only the flesh, consciously or unconsciously. They go their own way. And now the Savior is supposed to give help quickly. Whom would

He be helping then? Their ungodly flesh. So there are people who cannot obtain the slightest thing from God, because with their whole being they are so sure of themselves and are going so very wrong that God must think, "I will let them go their way. If I were to help them it would only be to their disadavantage and help them on their evil way, whether they see it or not. Though it cost my own honor among them, I cannot help them, even if they then say that there is no God."

Then again there are others who in a certain part of their being are closer to God's kingdom. God can find some good in them; so there is a bit of light. However, we should be aware of how cautious God has to be with regard to those whose lives justify Him only in part. All too easily God's gifts can be spoiled again in their flesh. Finally there are people who give themselves completely to God and only want God's good in themselves, be it through judgment. Here much can be given. So it was that Jesus Christ laid a foundation around himself, on which everything was possible. For He sought God's right and God's truth and gave himself even unto death, indeed unto death on the cross.

Him we must now follow. We are to be a kind of vanguard and ask in all our prayers with our whole hearts, **Thy kingdom come!** To begin with, we must somehow set up quarters for God's kingdom among us before we can come along with requests to God to make changes in this world for our sake. We must first ask ourselves to what extent God's kingdom is upheld in our surroundings. Do we let the Savior have a say in our affairs for the honor of God?

Depending on the answer, we may often have to stop praying and just be patient. I cannot constantly pray that my misery be taken from me. Often I see that it is more important simply to pray: Lord, take me into thy hands, so that thy rulership may be in me! Whoever has this attitude can have a place in God's kingdom.

This was the attitude of the men of God, the prophets and the apostles, who in ancient times fought for God's kingdom, and for whose sake God did great miracles. We too can attain something; but the kingdom of God must be much more in the foreground than it has been in the past. There is also a religiousness devoid of God's rule. We can even think that it is possible to please God by training ourselves in a certain holiness; whereas God does not find His right in us at all. Let us rather give God the honor and see to it that His kingdom can arrive in us; then we can achieve a lot. Then it is also possible to pray for others. Then one can dare to make requests and cry out to God for mercy and help, that there be light on our earth. Indeed, **one** man can become important for the whole world, if he has only God's kingdom in mind and not himself. We see this in Abraham. We know also how other men and apostles became important for all mankind by the way in which God manifested himself through them.

So it is possible that the prayer of one man may be answered while the prayer of another is not answered. Not that God has more love for the one man than for the other. For the moment, however, the one has drawn God's kingdom to himself and has made room for God in his life by denying his flesh and his earthly life. The other one has not done this. The one prays out of a concern for God's honor, the other out of pain and grief and because he wants help. God can give more to the man who may not be so clever, but who hungers and thirsts for the kingdom of God, than to one who wants to help God with great gifts; for the latter does not have God's kingdom. So very much depends on our trembling and shaking for God's kingdom even in good times, for God's right in us. We should not seek what is our own, but Jesus Christ alone. Otherwise the foundation will crumble as soon as the waves of suffering surge in like billows of water which threaten to drown us.

As yet we cannot see much of the foundation of God's kingdom in the world. Round about us there is not enough of the foundation of God's kingdom to plant anew the banner of Jesus Christ, the risen one. In the quiet of our hearts we can do it, but we are too weak to be a witness to the world. The world no longer believes. It does not even listen any more; it runs away from us Christians. Therefore God's kingdom must come with His deeds, a **new foundation** must be laid. So we must not rest or think we have it already. At most we are on the way, but we have not yet found the treasure. We do want to find it, if God gives us the strength we need, though it may cost our lives. We throw ourselves into the death of Jesus

Christ, and want to die so that He may live. If God Almighty meets us with His deathly sword, we will not flee. We will seek His honor with endurance and strength until His kingdom breaks in and Jesus Christ reveals himself in the glory of the Father through the Holy Spirit.

8
OUR JEHOVA

> I, Jehova, am the Lord your God who brought you out of the land of Egypt, out of the house of bondage. —Exodus 20, 2

These words stand at the beginning of the so-called Ten Commandments. They stand in the first place, like a rock, and all of God's will flows from them like a fresh, living spring. If we have the rock we also have the spring, the source; and our relationship to God becomes a true one. If we lose the rock we no longer have the source; and even if some of God's commandments may please us, they do not connect up with our lives, and God's life will not be truly glorified in us. Yet this is what we want to strive for all together; our whole being must become more true.

Many people nowadays think little of the Old Testament as compared to the New Testament. Yet when I read the Old Testament I am again and again struck by the story it tells. The guidance of God's Spirit in the men of God who from time to time appear in Israel always manifests itself sharply to the effect that in God's people everything must be true. There must not be merely a semblance of life as in other nations. There is to be no false honor in politics and culture, no false religion of forms, no forced, affected conduct. There must be no hypocrisy which through lies tries to deny what is natural, what is still imperfect on earth. Everything must be true and straightforward, in spite of the many faults and shortcomings Then God will help the upright to succeed.

This is the tone of all God's speaking in the Scripture. All the prophets struggle for truthfulness among the people, so that nothing hidden and covered up is lived before God. This truthfulness, this reverence for God's will, flows from the one rock Jehova. Nothing else shall influence the people of God: nothing else shall instill religious reverence in the people of God.

What does Jehova mean, the name in which Israel shall see God? This Jehova is something which has now appeared on earth, and which visibly and tangibly proves its working and being as God among men. Therefore the words follow, "who brought you out of the land of Egypt." Jehova is to be recognized in this miracle, in the miracle of the pillar of cloud and fire, in the manna, the bread of the desert, and in the water gushing forth from the rock, in all that is divine and invisible, and yet humanly visible and tangible. "This is your God!" the powerful voice calls, "the God who has delivered you and will deliver you also in the future, until you are delivered from all evil, if you hold on to Him." Thus the divine power in Israel also worked toward redemption and wanted to prepare the people for redemption. It was the will of God, Jehova, to live with His holy being amidst an earthly people. This justified the people in seeking redemption not merely in the liberation of men's souls from the bonds and fetters of lying and corruption in their midst. Rather, they were to expect that the earth around them, freed from the curse, might again become a fountain of blessing. Then Jehova would appear in the milk and honey of the earth, in all that lives thereon, just as He appeared in the pillar of cloud and fire. Through Israel the earth was to become God's land, a paternal heritage to the children who were to receive from it all the gifts of life.

This Jehova was to be expected from above and from below, from heaven and from earth. He was to be expected as the creator of heaven and earth. It is part of God's truth that man's life on earth must prove its divine origin in all directions. Our earthly life, our earthly toil and work, should be no less divinely true and justified than the inward movements of the spirit which rise to heaven in praise of God. We, in our day, can say that the fulfilment of God's kingdom lies in God's will being done on earth as in heaven.

The invisible, great God, the holy and exalted one, whose essence no man can grasp with his mind, unites with the earth in the name Jehova. In other words, "I am present and shall be wherever you are, and I am present in such a way that you can understand me." Thus the blessed community with God is brought about which distinguishes a true people of God from all other peoples. On the ground on which man is created and sustained, a communion is given with all the powers and gifts of God that are possible, both in man's spiritual life and in the life of nature and creation around him.

The other nations also had God and many names by which they tried to express God in their midst. However sincere their striving, they could find only a one-sided truth. On the whole these images of God, though born from their longings, led them away from God on the way of their lust, on the way of superstition and mere human passions. Neither their spiritual nor their material conceptions led to a true life with God. In Israel, for the first time, God was to become truth. From there He could become truth in other nations also. Other nations had turned God into a lie and their ruin revealed the lie of their gods. In the same way Israel was to reveal the truth of God in her life, in an increasingly glorified life.

This is very important for us too, if we want to become a people of God. Before anything else we must find the rock from which the will of God flows in a natural way. God's will determines our life; His will creates life. God appeared to us as the Jehova in Christ. We were to have Him not only in this name, but in a person who has become what we are — man. In Israel the most important thing was that Jehova was honored as God, although this was merely His name. For us the most important thing is to honor Jesus as God, although He appears to us in a human form like one man to another. Whatever else one may think, Jesus is the only reflection of God on the earth in a twofold way: He towers upward into the heavens for perceptions of truth in the Spirit. He leads downward into the earthly, human life for the understanding of life and growth on the earth, God's creation. Then the earth will shine through His creatures, just as the heavens shine.

What is God? However much we talk about God's nature, however many books we write about it, it will remain an unattainable concept. Whenever we try to grasp God's nature, to make it our own, as it were, it flees again before doubts that arise from the other side, and unclarties that we cannot overcome. To simple people we can say quite simply, "Look to Jesus Christ; here is God, here He is within reach." In Jesus Christ we become silent. His whole life and being has something soothing for us. In Him we may dismiss all theories about God. In a simple, childlike way we, like Mary, may sit at His feet to be regenerated by the true, divine life which flows out to us from Him. In it we want to submerge ourselves body and soul as quickly as possible in order that we may become like Him in truth and justice, in our relationship toward God and toward men.

Thus also Israel was to be soothed by the appearance of her Jehova. All further questions and speculations about God and the world, about the mysteries of men's fate, which appears to be tossed to and fro between good and evil, were to stop before the loud call, "Be calm! For I, Jehova, am your redeemer! And with redemption, with the experience of the new life which I bring to you, all enlightenment that you need will come." Thus we too rest in Jesus. This faith is a quiet contemplation of His life, filled with a heavenly expectation of redemption. Through Him who died and yet lives, this redemption shall now go much deeper and lead to sublime experiences that were not possible in the people of Israel. For in Jesus we see that even death can be overcome. A life is shown to us for which we had no longer hoped. Yet we long for it in the depth of our hearts. The watchword now is the life of the body in spite of death.

A new heaven, a new earth, is the goal toward which God wants to lead us through Christ, on the way of redemption. In this we must become faithful. We must no longer go our own ways and think that God's goal can be reached with our religious institutions, usages and traditions. Our redemption will come only through God who in Christ again and again reveals himself and shows himself on earth as the living one. In Him we must give ourselves up. For His sake we must count everything else as loss, and surrender ourselves to be a true and just tool of His revelation.

This is faith, a faith that justifies us, placing us before God whose justice and truth can then be revealed in us. Christ gave himself in the flesh and in the corruption of the flesh. His death became a sacrifice before God, that we might find in Him the way to sacrifice ourselves as He did; that dying with Him we might become a people of life on earth, in uprightness, justice and holiness.

This is not just a teaching, intended for our momentary edification. On the contrary, all that I have tried to say in my weakness should make practical people of us, people full of zeal to win this Jesus. We should strive to become a people free of ourselves and of our traditions. Then we shall be able truly to serve God for the redemption. It is a real shame to see the diverse forms of Christianity for which many people give their lives in our time. Just as the heathens sacrifice to their false gods, so today there are many Christians who sacrifice to falsities created by the Christian religion — not by Christ. Even honest people find it hard to break away and to follow the words, "I, God, am your God in Jesus, in nothing else whatever its name may be." We must find this rock in these words of God. Then the fountains of truth will flow for us. Then our lives will also become true. The lives of most Christians have become just as false in God's eyes as the lives of most Israelites who in ancient times practiced idolatry and later their own brand of piety. One's own piety can become a god just as false as the gods of heathens.

If we want to fight for the kingdom of God, then it might be more important and more necessary to do away with the nine tenths of all Christian religion that has become false. Thus we would come upon the simple rock which is Christ alone, bare and unadorned though it may appear. Then the Savior himself could live and rule, instead of the many rulerships that come from men while pretending to be from God. Therefore we should not have so many qualms about traditional things which in any case are no longer true. God will show himself to the upright, even if they are not able to follow the grandiose spiritual leaders and theologians. We must become true toward God and toward men, as Jesus was true. No other god shall rule over us. Then we shall come upon the rock on which there is a fellowship that can be called blessed, because it is a fellowship with God and with one another. Such a fellowship no longer places any obstacles in the way of redemption.

Let us allow these things to ripen in us. Then we all shall experience in our lives that our Jehova — Jesus — lives and rules, praised and glorified in all eternity.

9

THE LIGHT OF THE WORLD

Today the words of Jesus came to me, **"I am the light of the world."** These words we want to consider today. It is comforting that He does not say, "I am your light," or "I am the light of a nation," or "I am the light of a church," or even "I am the light of my disciples." No, He says, "I am the light of **the world.**" The Savior obviously wants to tell us something which comes to us from many other parts of the Bible. "Don't draw me into all your petty affairs. It is as though you were sticking in a glue pot, like a fly sticking to honey, and couldn't get rid of it. Don't draw me into your nature. Nobody should think that I have come only to him, and that I now have to wash only his feet and shine his boots. No, accept me as the one who has come to the whole world, through whom the world has been created. I am the one who sustains the world and who will create a new world. Through me the Father and Creator of all worlds speaks to you. Unless you take me in this way, I will remain far from you."

This is what is meant, dear friends, when it is said that "Christ came into the flesh." It is a pity that Christianity has exploited these sublime words — "come into the flesh, come into the world"—in a selfish way. This is probably the reason for the shadow which is cast over all Christendom. We remain without Jesus, without the one who says, "I am the light of the world," if we remain in this petty, selfish attitude in which everyone has his own "dear Savior," and cooks himself a nice sweet pudding to eat comfortably to his heart's content. In this way we don't become children of God, truly generous. We don't get out of our own nature; we don't really know how to live in a way worthy of God. We remain always the same mean and miserable people, stirring around in our own nature. So we go to pieces and finally complain to heaven that God does not care about us. Certainly God does not care about your selfish interests. He came into the world. If you want to meet the Savior, then you must go out into the world, leaving behind your personal concerns. Don't stay in one corner. Be on your guard against your own pettiness and seek the world. There you will find Jesus.

Of course I don't mean that world which is penetrated by sin and death. That is a false world. Jesus says, "I come into God's creation. I am here to serve this creation of God, so that God's will may be done, and that one day it may be as in the beginning: And God saw everything that He had made, and behold, it was **very good.**" (Gen. 1, 31) We have to find the way into this creation.

One would think that this is very easy, but in fact it is very difficult. We are surrounded by the creation. We draw our breath from it. We draw our whole life, down into the smallest things, from creation. We are bound and fettered to it. We cannot imagine anything else but ourselves and creation, creation and ourselves. We have to draw every breath from creation, or else our life ceases. It is God's goodness which nourishes us continually from the creation. And yet we cannot enter into creation, into the true, pure, divine nature.

It is a desperate situation. Try to introduce only a little bit of natural life into society; it won't work. The human race must have something artificial, something affected, that twists man and distorts his features. You cannot just be yourself if you want to be an educated person. This goes for heathens and Christians alike. It is the same everywhere. You need something false, otherwise you are not educated. It is like a curse, a human curse. It grips us with iron claws and we cannot get free from it to enter into creation. And if we do try to escape this curse, there is a hue and cry just as with our Savior. He, who is the light of the world, in the end only heard people crying out, "Crucify him, crucify him!"

So it has remained to this day. Whenever one attempts to attack the human spirit that tries to separate us from creation, one hears, "Crucify him!" Yet those who do not want to take this fight upon themselves, are no helpers of God and the Lord Jesus. So today, my friends, I do not want to tell you that Jesus is your helper. For in fact He has been your helper for a long time; but now He waits for you to become His helpers. You should not fear this "Crucify!" when it is urgent that you stand up for truth and justice, which are part of creation.

We especially, in our household, have come together to take our responsibility upon ourselves. We want to let the other side of God's promise take second place, His promise for our redemption. Many have been offended by this attitude. Nevertheless, if people don't understand us, this need not hinder us. We have only to fortify in ourselves the will to take upon ourselves the duties that are ours if we want to follow Jesus Christ. We have to declare war on the **human world,** in ourselves and in others, in order to enter **the world of God;** not into heaven, for this is not our business in the first place. No, here on the earth, here is the creation which we are allowed to enter if only we are prepared. Here it is that the creation lies open before our eyes, the creation into which Jesus Christ, the victorious king, will lead us. To do this we must will as God wills. We must not be obstinate and spoil the whole work of Jesus Christ and construct a Christianity according to our own ideas. This will never lead us anywhere. We can see that today, two thousand years later, we are stuck in the same pettiness, in the same sins, in the same misery as all the other people. This is proof of the fact that we have not understood God's will. Or do you think God would have left mankind in its misery for such a long time, if there had been a people who grasped the sublime appearance of Jesus Christ in creation? John was quite right in saying, "He came into His own, and the people received Him not." Like a light He shone into the darkness, and the darkness did not accept Him to this day. But this must change! The darkness will yet have to accept Him. And if all the darknesses do not will it, then we must say to them in the name of the almighty God that they have to accept Him yet. You too, man, you must one day accept Jesus Christ and give Him the honor.

This, my friends, should be the concern of our hearts today. It is your duty to be God's helpers, and you will perish miserably if you do not want to help. Long enough you have called on the Savior for His help. He has done His duty from the beginning; you need not remind Him. Now it is your turn to stand by Him and to do something to help Him! I say this also for myself: We want to stand by the Lord Jesus. Let the whole world cry, "Crucify him!" We know that they crucified Him, but it did not harm Him. Let them also be crucified who help the Lord Jesus, who break away from human nature to enter into creation. Let them be crucified. They will yet live and come to no harm.

Now the first step in giving ourselves to this task is to recognize where we ourselves stand in the way. We must get out of the way if God is to be a light in this world. We should not step in and become a hindrance. No, we must be the first who are ready to sacrifice ourselves and to give ourselves with all that is of our own nature. With this will to sacrifice we come together on this day. We want to give ourselves for whatever God demands of us. You know well that a task has also been given to my house. We should all work together so as not to protect ourselves in a wrong way. For God's sake we must give ourselves up and break away from our past life, in so far as it was a wrong life. This is my wish; may God help us in this. Then each one will be able to contribute something for his part to prepare a way for God in Jesus Christ. Then He will no longer be hindered by us in caring for His creation.

A second step must follow. If we dedicate ourselves, my friends, then we must recognize our sins. When God's fire burns and the flames leap up against us and consume our human nature, this means repentance. Quite a different, more thorough repentance will be demanded of those who want to sacrifice themselves. Only in this way will our innermost flesh be given over to judgment and die in order that Jesus may live.

So we must take to heart, first, the willingness to sacrifice ourselves; and then in our surrender the readiness to endure in repentance until the judgments are fulfilled, until God has completed in us His will which He has demanded of us. Then, my friends, we shall also see that Jesus is the light of the **world**. Then He will come in radiance over all peoples of the earth. There will be a rejoicing amongst the peoples and amongst the nations as never before.

We have no inkling yet of what the world will be, what the nations will be, what creation will be, once Jesus Christ comes to fulfil that for which He was sent by the Father in heaven. As yet everything seems to be withheld. All the greatness, the sublime and creative power given in Jesus appears now like a pent-up stream of God's patience which wants to overcome the hidden powers of darkness. Now the time has come when the stream of God's glory surges forward to break through. Now is the last hour, the hour of decision: Is Jesus the light of the world, or is He not? And it shall be decided; He shall manifest Himself as the light of the world. Men shall fall at His feet weeping, and ask forgiveness for their unbelief.

In this way, my friends, let us unite today in the presence of God and do what is asked of us. Let each one of us carry in his heart the awareness of his duty to be a helper, so that the creation may once more become God's. Let each one of us feel worthy to surrender himself to the will and the plan of God in Jesus Christ, so that this Jesus, the light of the world, may come and wipe out the stain of death and sin in God's creation.

10
GOD'S KINGDOM

Some of them wanted to arrest him, but no one laid hands on him. The officers then went back to

GOD'S KINGDOM 143

> the chief priests and Pharisees, who said to them, "Why did you not bring him?" The officers answered, "No man ever spoke like this man!" The Pharisees answered them, "Are you led astray, you also? Have any of the authorities or of the Pharisees believed in him? But this crowd, who do not know the law, are accursed." Nicodemus, who had gone to him before, and who was one of them, said to them, "Does our law judge a man without first giving him a hearing and learning what he does?" They replied, "Are you from Galilee too? Search and you will see that no prophet is to rise from Galilee." So they went each to his own house.
>
> —John 7, 44-53

The words we have just heard are merely a brief comment on an episode in Jesus' life. Yet it is very important for us. The history of Jesus' life is the history of God's Kingdom then and now, and the same questions arise. It is the same argument about God's cause today as it was then. Some people are shaken; they feel something. Something grips their hearts — they themselves don't know how. It is the divine, the spiritual nature of Jesus. Then they submit, saying, "No man ever spoke like Jesus." Even if they don't understand it, there is nothing they can do against this man. The others hear only what they themselves think. They compare it to what Jesus says. Their hearts are hardened. They do not even notice that there is something special about it. And finally they say, "Search and you will see that no prophet is to arise from Galilee."

Also today we are concerned with the kingdom of

God, though I know well that for many it has drifted into the background. In our times people are aroused by many issues; their outward life makes great demands on them. More than at any other time, it would seem, man raises himself powerfully in his human search and progress. It is as though the whole world wanted to offer its forces to men, saying, "Use me; become great, become strong, become rich, creative, active — take everything into your hands!" Forces which earlier times hardly dreamed of are now opened up for us. Everybody finds himself in the position to make use of these new inventions and these new forces for his own purposes. Man's whole earthly life depends on this. If he were to shut his eyes to these things, he would lag behind and finally perish in his earthly life. There is a spirit of intellectual accomplishment that pushes the concern for God's kingdom to one side, so that one no longer knows quite what it is all about.

It must however be said by way of justification that as time passed a tremendous misunderstanding came about, precisely with regard to this speaking of God's kingdom. Much has been said about the church. Much has been said about the teachings which are preserved in the church, about confessions that have become a sacred good within the body of Christianity. Too much emphasis has been placed on formalities by which we prove ourselves as Christians before other people. Now all forms have become obsolete, superannuated as it were. Today we cannot deny that many people no longer really find the living qualities that our Father in heaven wanted to give us in Jesus Christ. People are so tired of hearing the same things over and over again that they often do not know what course to take. Yet they have neither seen nor experienced the life that comes from God. So they are in a fix. On the one hand they cannot deny that "we too need God, God's word, God's revelation, in our hearts." On the other hand they no longer quite believe in the means through which God's word is being preached to us at present. This is why many no longer know what to do with themselves in regard to God's kingdom. Their hearts hunger and thirst; they are aware that something of God's eternity and truth should become revealed in us, but they don't quite know what to do about it.

Just because of all this we must begin to speak of God's kingdom in a new way. In spite of present-day conditions, where much of the church and of Christian fellowship is almost dead, we can speak of God's kingdom to men of our time. The kingdom of God is and was and will be the rulership of justice, of order, of power, of law, of all that is of God in creation. This, my friends, is what moves us men, and this must come into being. For unless our lives are molded according to this rulership, we shall ever remain dissatisfied. In spite of all the achievements of our time we shall not be able to boast of one single advantage in our lives. We may find conveniences, but the revival of the eternal things in you, O man, will be smothered unless God's being in His eternal rules and laws, in

His truth and in His justice, dawns in you as the light of life.

Yet this very thing, my friends, causes much discord as soon as it is voiced again. We should not deceive ourselves even in our time. Millions of people can be Christians in all peace and comfort from childhood on until they are laid in the grave. They are satisfied with what is said about God, and it does not make them feel uncomfortable in any way. Religion is taken as part of one's life; one accepts it such as it is. This causes no conflict, or at the most an argument about the interpretation of this or that teaching, but these arguments are futile. A new conflict arises as soon as we feel urged once more to proclaim the kingdom of God as something living. This is what I want to do among you today. I don't just want to edify you. Rather I want to call out to you what God has laid in my heart: God's kingdom is a living kingdom and government, and even today it is at hand. I would like to go still further and say that today it is closer at hand than we may think. The intervention of the living God in mankind can be more powerful today than many believe. It is my firm conviction that we live in a time when God wants to manifest himself as the one who **is** something and who **does** something. He is the God with whom we should joyfully concern ourselves so that our lives may remain His and may be glorified in His honor.

In speaking of God's kingdom, we proclaim that Jesus Christ has not died. He is not someone who appeared 2000 years ago, to be viewed as a personality of the past about whom we retain certain recollections and teachings. No, just as Jesus lived 2000 years ago, He lives today. Today He wants to triumph in our midst for the honor of God. He wants to be the living one so that among us the reverence for the Father in heaven may grow and deepen. Man must come before God and in the weakness and poverty of his nature raise his eyes to the Father in heaven, with a sigh in his heart, saying, "My Father, my Father, I too want to be your child!" Then he may believe with life-giving strength: Jesus lives, He will help me, He is victor, He breaks down my resistance. Whoever I may be, even if I were the most wretched human being, covered with shame — even I am found worthy of being called a child of the Father. Even I am allowed to go forward to meet God's kingdom, so that His name may be sanctified in me and His government may break in; so that His will may be done in me just as it is done in heaven!

I wish, my friends, that I could place in your hearts the living power of our God and Savior. I wish that I could help you to understand that this living power makes new men of us. It overcomes some of our misery, even in our physical life. Our earthly conditions must become more truthful, more sublime, more just. God's living power seeks us out and wants to show us in the midst of the entanglements of life a clear, true value which makes nobler men of us. Then we shall no longer be dependent on every fate that befalls us. We shall no longer be humiliated when earthly evil lays hold on us. We will hold high our heads, for we will be men able to conquer in the spirit of our heavenly Father all that still needs to be conquered here on earth.

I wish that I could make all this quite clear to you. For it is true that there are many things still to be overcome, visible and invisible things. In the invisible realm of man's own nature there is more resistance to God's truth than people believe. In human society, in all the influences to which we are exposed, there lies a hindrance to the living power of our Lord Jesus Christ, and this hindrance is greater than people suspect. I often find that I can talk and discuss the teachings of God, of Christ, of the Holy Spirit, and agree with people. Nobody is annoyed by this. The conflict begins, however, as soon as I take a firm stand and say, "My friends, I have experienced who Jesus is. I have looked into the living power, into the kingdom of our God which even today wants to take hold of us. I tell you that even now the truth and the life-power of our God is at work. I declare to you that even now the truth of God's kingdom comes visibly to this earth. We do not have to wait until we lay ourselves down to die and be buried. Here and now we can hear with our ears, see with our eyes, who Jesus is, who the life-giving Spirit is. It is the same today as at the time of the apostles. Today also there are prophets and apostles who say, 'Watch out; the kingdom of heaven is really at hand.' It is not a question of this or that church, of this or that teaching, but alone of Jesus Christ himself. With Him we have to come to terms."

For me this is the one and only direction. Yet if

I say all this, then there is an argument. "Who is this arrogant person? How can anyone say such things? Are the Bible and the confessions not enough for us? Is it necessary to come along with things long past? This is superstition and exaggeration!" So there is a conflict, but it is a holy conflict. It kindles a light in many hearts, a light of hope, a light of strength, a light from the heights beyond this earth. Nothing can give us more strength than the certainty that Jesus lives, that He does something, that He is not an empty word. In saying His name we are stirred by these words out of His life, "He who believes in me, as the Scripture has said, 'out of his heart shall flow rivers of living water'." (John 7, 38) Nothing gives more strength than the knowledge that Jesus is in our midst. This we are to believe, so that His essence may become true in us, so that His Spirit may purify us.

What then does it mean to believe, since the time Jesus came to the world? There is much dispute about belief; but woe to us, I tell you frankly, woe to us and our arguments about faith! Isn't it something quite simple, that every child can understand? My friends, if Jesus truly lives, if He is to be your King, then you must no longer take anything into your own hands. Then you must deny yourself in all things that are God's. You must be a dying man, one who in things of God says, "Here I can do nothing. Hands off what is God's, what is Jesus Christ's. For none but Jesus has the right to make a decision in divine matters!" In this way we believe; in this way we honor this King.

You can do much in earthly things, for you have

understanding with which you can and should arrange your life and live in a sensible manner. God's things, however, those things which have to do with God's kingdom, are Jesus Christ's concern. If God's kingdom is important to you, then you need not think you have to be anything important. Rather you should place yourself at Jesus' feet, thinking, "I am a weak human being, but Jesus lives, Jesus is victor. To Him I will give myself, and in my heart I will turn everything over to Him so that nothing can rule over me but He alone." This is faith.

Therefore I would like to call out into the world, "Die, that Jesus may live!" In other words, do not attach any importance to what is false, to what is opposed to truth, to what must be given into death by you yourselves; for this is our business. We must recognize in faith that Jesus Christ is the Lord. We must raise our fists — so to speak — against all that comes from the flesh, from the deceitfulness of our own thinking. Indeed I wish for you an iron fist against all that is untrue and wrong. Do it for the sake of your God, your Savior! Get up and beat it down! What is false shall be called false. What is wrong shall die and die again, and die so that it no longer counts for anything, not even the least little bit. So let us be fighters for God's sake, for Jesus Christ's sake! The eternal shall live; Jesus shall live and rule for the glory of God the Father. This is how you should understand the words, "Die, and Jesus will live!" He is our Master, our Lord and King, who will reveal himself in God's majesty when His time has come. Then we shall be amazed at how much is possible through His government.

If we are believers in Jesus Christ, then, we must hold on to these things in defiance of the whole world. May the Spirit of the living God strike our hearts and make these things come true in us. It will be of no use to you to have heard a man speak, to believe in a doctrine, or to sacrifice yourselves to anything else. All this will be of no avail to you. But it will help you to become prophets gripped by the spirit of God, if you are moved for your God, for your Father, for Jesus, the Lord and Savior, who is and was and shall be.

11

PEOPLE OF ZION

> Listen to me, my people, and give ear to me, my nation; for a law will go forth from me, and my justice for a light to the peoples.
> —Isaiah 51, 4

This whole chapter of the book of Isaiah is addressed to the people of Zion. Actually one should simply read it and add nothing to it, except perhaps to make a psalm out of it which one could then sing straight away. But people are so little used to taking seriously what is written about Zion that something has to be said in order to help them understand it.

In Zion everyone is concerned with **justice**. Zion is something different from Christianity. Christians only look for grace; the people of Zion look for justice — that is the difference. In Zion the whole nation wants judgment and justice — this is the joy of Zion's people. They do not seek any good for themselves, but only God's justice. In the midst of struggle and strife, of much pain right and left, it is a comfort to see that God's right and justice are victorious.

These are the people of Zion. They don't think of themselves at all. Their own life is quite unimportant to them, at least in the sense in which it is important to other people. Our life has no meaning in itself; it has meaning only in relation to God. I do not want to live unless I am a servant of God. If God suffers, I too want to suffer. If God is reviled, I too want to be reviled. If He has no joy, then neither do I want to have joy. If God's life cannot flourish, then I do not want my life to prosper either. In Zion no one is interested in himself; everyone's concern is that in God's creation things shall go according to His purpose.

For the people of Zion still regard the earth as God's creation. They are far from thinking that the earth is a vale of tears. All they know is that men are miserable, and unfortunately have brought things to such a point that they are unhappy in the midst of a splendid creation. The people of Zion shake with fury if someone says that the earth is so evil that it is impossible to carry on. They will tell you that the evil is in your heart. All the evil in the world is men's fault, down into the smallest things, even the weather. It is quite clear that God has nothing whatever to do with bad weather, except that in all fairness He gives us what we deserve. If we are gloomy, unclear people, things must become gloomy also round about us.

Zion's people even rejoice in the judgments God sends us to make us realize what we are, for only by the judgments can we appraise ourselves.

The man of Zion has to do only with God. His only concern is what is fruitful for God. Thus we too should think in times of distress: What of it? If we are faithful in our hearts, then God will be able to make use of us even in times when things are not going so well for us. For we are called to work with Him, not against Him. Not only when we are joyful and gay can we do this, but also when we want to weep with God over the sins of the world. To make it easier for us, He sent His Son into our midst to bear the sins of the world. Him we can follow; to Him we can offer our shoulders to help carry the guilt. This is our duty.

People don't want to do this either in the visible or in the invisible world. This is why the comfort which we already have in our hearts does not come to them. For God calls to us, "I comfort Zion! Be patient, I am the Lord, Jehova. If you are faithful, a great day of justice and truth will dawn!" This call is our only comfort. We cannot be comforted with a fool's paradise or with the promise to take us into heaven. That is no comfort to us. Only God can comfort us when He takes things into His hands. If I were to come into heaven today and God were to say to me, "Now you have a nice place," I would answer, "No, I am not satisfied! How can I be satisfied if you do not have what is rightfully and justly yours?" Only justice and right can comfort us. Nothing else can possibly sustain the people of Zion. So finally even a time of judgment becomes a time of joy.

This means, of course, that one must have a certain relationship with God. This is very necessary; yet it is probably missing with many people. But whose fault is it if the contact with God is lost? Who is responsible for the fact that very few believers know what Jesus thinks at this moment? We don't know anything about it. What is He thinking? We chatter about God and Jesus, but it makes me feel somehow embarrassed. Just imagine He were listening; He might well say, "Be quiet, you don't even know what I am thinking and saying today; you have no contact with me!" The fact that we have no real relationship with God is extremely serious. Yet this relationship is all I want.

As for myself, all the sermons in the world could stop right now, if someone were to say instead, "I know what is going on in heaven, and of this I tell!" No human being knows it, and therefore there are no **witnesses.** The fact that our relationship to God's kingdom, our public relationship with God, has stopped, is the greatest judgment we have to bear at present.

That was the great thing with the apostles; they did have a contact with God. I cannot understand how people today can maintain that they are entitled just as much as the apostles to preach the gospel in the whole world. I cannot possibly agree with them. You do not have the same rights; not at all! You may do some good, but to be able to do it with the real power in which the apostles did it, one must at least have a relationship with God.

I cannot just embrace the Catholic or the Lutheran faith; I cannot just be a Pietist or a Baptist. These things don't make a relationship with God; He is quite indifferent to them. It is as though someone were to bring me water saying, "This water comes from the Lake of Constance, and this other from the Zurich lake." What do I care? Water is water, whatever lake it comes from. Neither does God care about our confessions. The very fact that we call ourselves Catholics or Lutherans as though we were doing this in God's name, is the clearest proof that we have no contact with God. I would like to shake the world out of this delusion whereby people think that they are God's because they belong to a certain party. God's iron broom has to sweep out all these fabrications. Unless we seek a true relationship with God, unless we seek God's justice, we have no right to God's kingdom and shall never know comfort.

Should we mourn over this? No, it should be our greatest joy! Therefore I am able to preach the overall, great reconciliation which goes through the whole of creation. Every church condemns what does not belong to it. Our faith, however, is not tied to a dogma, but binds us to the one God who is God to **all men.** Whether you call yourself Christian or Mohammedan, I tell you, you are just as much God's as I am. You Gentile and you Jew are just as much God's as I am — for you are all men. You are a man and should be proud of it, because this comes from

God. You should not be proud of your religion, for this comes from men. Who wants to contradict me? My body and my life come from God. Do my books and my teachings come from God? No, indeed! Only what I have of Jesus comes from God. And Jesus is not contained in any book. Jesus is life, Jesus is resurrection, Jesus leads to the living God. We have no need to force ourselves into any human structure.

Thus on the one hand the situation is very serious. It is a shame that people no longer really want and value the relationships with God; instead they seek relationships with men. On the other hand it is a joy that all our human religions are failing. You will see how everything that we set up in God's place will fall into the dust. The time must come at last when we shall accept God himself. He who alone is ruler, the almighty God through Jesus Christ, will be placed on the throne. Whoever wants to set up anything else will perish. For in this world none other than Jesus Christ shall one day rule for the honor of God the Father.

This is a comfort. This means reconciliation. All men must rejoice in it. No one shall say any more that he is lost. The churches have brought things to the point where millions of people despair, saying, "I am lost." Yet he who has found a relationship to God's kingdom can never say, "I am lost." Even if he were sitting in hell, he should always be able to say, "Reconciliation will come, and in His blood I too shall be reconciled, for I am God's." It is true that reconciliation will come through justice and in the blood of Jesus Christ, and I have to surrender to the judgment. However, I must never again say that I am lost and that I am not of God. It is the greatest sin to doubt that you, as man, are God's. Every creature is God's and any doubt of this is a grave sin. All your other sins are nothing compared to this one sin, to doubt that you are God's. Even in the lowest regions of hell you can still hold on to the knowledge, "I am God's!" Finally hell will be forced open with this certainty. If you cling to Jesus, you will be saved and belong to those who even in their deepest sorrow know that mankind may perish, yet God's justice is everlasting.

12
THE CHURCH OF JESUS CHRIST

Now when Jesus came into the district of Caesarea Philippi, he asked his disciples, "Who do men say that the Son of man is?" And they said, "Some say John the Baptist, others say Elijah, and others Jeremiah, or one of the prophets." He said to them, "But who do you say that I am?" Simon Peter replied, "You are the Christ, the Son of the living God." And Jesus answered him, "Blessed are you, Simon Bar-Jona! For flesh and blood has not revealed this to you, but my Father who is in heaven. And I tell you, you are Peter, and on this rock I will build my church, and the powers of death shall not prevail against it. I will give you the keys of the kingdom of heaven, and whatever you bind on earth is bound in heaven, and whatever you loose on earth is loosed in heaven."

—Matthew 16, 13-19

This is a description of how God's kingdom comes into this world like a mustard seed. Here is Jesus, the Son of Man, more real man than any other man, more childlike than all other children. He lives among men and He is the kingdom of God. He does not make it; He **is** the kingdom! Why? Because He is God and man. When God created the world He founded His kingdom on earth. The earth was His kingdom. And who was to reign, to rule and to watch over it as His representative? **Man.** God's kingdom was in paradise through man. God's kingdom is on earth through one upright man, no matter what men are like otherwise. The contrast between good and evil, between light and darkness in the world, makes no difference. One true man — and God's kingdom is here! What did this contrast amount to in paradise? What were light and darkness, life and death, the serpent and God's justice? They amounted to nothing, nothing at all. An Adam, and there it was, God himself in paradise. Even if here and there something wrong was still lurking in corners, that didn't matter. A man was there, and God was with this man. Nothing else was of any importance. Indeed, it dissolved, as sugar dissolves in water, before this one man, Adam.

The loss of man was the world's catastrophe. Man was gone. This is still the world's undoing today. Yet now we do have the fortune to know that there is one in whom the world is God's again, in whom all that is created is again placed into the light of the first creation. This one is Jesus. Where then is evil, death, corruption? Jesus is here! In His presence, what is there to fear? Suffering and corruption, night and death, disappear. Where He comes, men are set free as long as Jesus is among them. Through Him the desert is turned into paradise, the sick are healed, the dead come alive, the poor become rich, the foolish clever. The down-trodden and broken are raised up and praise God. Everything is allowed to come back to life. Man is present again in God's creation; God's creation breathes and shines forth again in one Man, Jesus.

It is then that the question is asked, "Who do men say that the Son of Man is?" People guess one way or another and don't see who He is. Maybe John, maybe Elijah, or maybe Jeremiah? They don't see it. In Jesus, paradise and the first creation were there again. Yet for people to see this, to recognize that He is a man, a man of God, they need divine inspiration. They seek high and low and do not find the answer. It is as though the spirits of confusion besieged them, perplexing their minds. They all have lofty thoughts, Biblical thoughts, and in their imagination think of all sorts of ways that God's kingdom must come. The simplest thing, however, which God does and must do so that all may be saved, they cannot see: God again sends a Man.

If the Savior were to come today, He would surely come as a man. The world needs a man. God was always there; He was in the world before Jesus. God ruled everything from Adam until Jesus. The Creator never separated himself from His work, never.

But true man, through whom creation can really become God's and as such be influenced, ruled, protected and cultivated — true man was missing. He is still missing and will be missing until Jesus comes and does away with the false man. The false man is the world's undoing. It is not true that there is no God; however, because there are so many false men, one no longer sees the Father in heaven. It is not true that there is no Spirit of God who made the world; but the false spirits destroy everything. It is this false nature which at present comes to the fore in mankind. There are so many false men that one no longer sees true man. Thus creation is concealed, at least superficially. False men with a false spirit, with false desires and false aims, think that they are real men. Yet they are unhappy, because in reality they are false men. Wherever true man is, there is heaven on earth. Let us become true men in our congregation at Boll or in any other little parish. Then paradise will be here! We don't need a special heaven for this; our earth is beautiful enough! But there must be true men on it. Then paradise is here.

Jesus was such a man. He was crucified, rejected, despised, because He was true man and wanted to have nothing to do with the false spirits of His time. He did not care about the emperor and the authorities, although He was very courteous towards them. He did not care about the temple, although He preached in it. He did not care for the arts and the various institutions, although He allowed these things freely to exist. He did not care for science and philosophy, but neither did He attack them. He was a man who cared only for God. People took offense at all this, and therefore they nailed Him to the cross. Now He is gone. Now we seem to have lost paradise once more because He is gone.

It is true that they were apparently able to get rid of Him by crucifying Him. Now the fight is carried on in the invisible realm. Yet the crucified one will not be pushed aside for ever. Now Jesus seeks a **living church,** and He seeks it on the earth. Could not the one who rose from the dead have come quickly, in heavenly glory, to conquer and overcome all things? He would have done it long ago, without hesitating, if this would have made God's kingdom possible. He could have come with hosts of angels. But no! He doesn't want only angels. Man, not super-worldly powers, must serve God on earth. True man must do it, and God must do it in him. This is Jesus' loyalty towards us false men. He could have come in judgment. For a time people even thought He would come in this way and smash up everything in the last judgment. If He had wanted to come in judgment, He could have destroyed the false men already 2000 years ago. Why wait another 2000 years if they are to be damned in any case? No, it isn't like this. No, no! Jesus does not want to kill us; He has never wanted to do this. He would rather wait another 1000 years, if need be, than give us up. This is Jesus Christ's faithfulness, that He is patient. Through Him we are to become real men once more, and through true men the Father in heaven will come to us.

Peter was the first to confess openly, "You, Jesus, Son of Man, you are God's Son, the Son of the living God. We want to go nowhere else — where should we go? You are the one, you alone! We need you. Through you we have the Father in heaven. What else do we need but you, the Son of Man? You are the kingdom of God!" We too must come to this point, in order that Jesus Christ's thirst for men may be quenched. At present Jesus does not come into His rulership — the false men do not come to Jesus. Do not be deceived. Every acre of earth is still covered with false men, to put it crudely. Hundreds of times Christianity was deceived and took false forms for the real thing. But falsities shall not prevail; the false men must come to an end. The true, genuine man will live and triumph. His is the earth, the sky, and His are all men. It is indeed a great thing, my friends, if in the midst of this dreadful confusion of false nature, false spirits and false men, even one person rises to say, **"You are the one.** I no longer want any part of the world. You, Jesus, are the one." Then Jesus is comforted; then we too are comforted. For if one man is able to say it, if the light can dawn in one man, then there is hope that in others too the light will dawn. When that happens, then the church of God arises.

This is the rock on which Jesus founds His church: "You, Peter, are this rock. Yet it is not you who are the rock, but my Father. He revealed it to you. In you the light of the living God dawned, and this binds you to me. In this way you too are a child of the living God, for in you the Father can speak." Now we know how the church of Jesus Christ comes into being.

Some people think they can found a church of Jesus Christ by cutting themselves off from the world and sitting in a corner. That won't do at all. Just try it! You would be taking the false man along with you. For one thousand years men have tried to do it. It was all in vain; the way was wrong. Other people think they have managed when they have picked a quarrel with the church, but that is no good either. You can found as many sects as you like; it will lead you nowhere. I do not make light of the striving of many people who are willing to deny themselves for God's sake. There are people who in their grief over sin have never permitted themselves a single laugh, a single pleasure, not even the joy of contemplating nature. I respect their serious outlook. Yet believe me — this is not the right way. On this way there will never be a church of Jesus Christ.

The church of Jesus Christ is to be the light of creation, of the existing world, of our skies; it is to be a light in the clouds, in the atmosphere, even under the earth. Jesus is truly Lord over the whole creation, and God's kingdom penetrates all that is created. His church is to have the width and breadth of Jesus, of God, of all creation. The light which Jesus kindles in His church must be as great as the Father, for the Father alone gives His church to the Savior.

How then does this church come into being? Those who have seen Jesus must really stop letting themselves be distracted from the revelation of the

Father. They should cease to seek Christ through theology and Christian dogma. They must no longer try to make God's kingdom with worldly powers or even with spiritual powers. You may laugh at me! I will gladly be a fool in the eyes of the whole world; I ask nothing of you. For God's kingdom I ask nothing but revelation. Unless God moves my heart, unless the Father opens my eyes to Jesus, I will get nowhere. I may become a good man; but God's kingdom, God's church, can be founded only on the rock which the Father in heaven himself revealed.

On this rock I want to stand and defend the Savior to the last drop of my blood. I cannot live in any other way. In this I have my gladness and my rejoicing, and therefore I call out to the false nature of mankind, "Get out of the way! Stop your doings!" The time will come when all that hinders the church will become quite small. The false men will have to be silent. We men cannot make it; only the Father can. We want to be in it with our whole mind, our whole heart and our whole strength, and say, "If only I have the Father and you have Him; if only two of us are united for Christ, then He who is Lord over the earth will be with us." Who can then prevail against us? Then it is no longer we who do anything; then it is the Father and the man Jesus Christ, the light of creation in heaven and on the earth and beneath the earth. **He** will found the living church. We do not want to make anything. We do not want to spend our strength in organizing meetings, in theories, science, art, politics. We want none of all this. Once people gather together, even only a handful, and stand on the rock which is the Father in heaven, then the realities of God's kingdom will appear.

Do not think that God's cause can just fall from heaven. There has to be a living church. The Savior says expressly, "To you I will give the keys of the kingdom, to you man in whom my Father lives." It is given into the hands of men in whom the Father lives to bind and to loose on earth so that it is valid also in heaven. What such men do on earth is also valid in heaven. Yet the Father must be fully in them, else it amounts to nothing. It is a great mistake to think that every theologian, every pastor, can loose and bind. The light of our heavenly Father must be in a man, but not a false light. It is not the ministry appointed by us men that has the keys in hand. It is not where we select people, where we examine them. We do not hand the keys of the kingdom to men. Only one who receives God's revelation can be a man who looses or releases. Any farmer, any woman, can be a person who releases. If a person stands on a rock, he can release. The living church of Christ may be made up of poor, simple, little people; it will yet be able to loose and set free. Then the powers of God's kingdom and its realities are at work on the earth, in heaven, and beneath the earth; they are at work because Jesus lives through the will of the almighty God. My friends, you should rejoice that our earth is valued in this way! Jesus said that **on earth** things shall be bound and loosed.

"Whatever you bind and loose on earth — **on**

the earth — is valid with our Father in heaven!" Here is this poor planet Earth, this little heap of dust. Yet what clarity, what majesty, is given when there is a true man, when the Son of Man gathers men around himself, men who also are sons, sons of the Father, sons of the living God. Then God and man will become one on earth; then the Father is on the earth. I wish, my friends, that you could feel the greatness of what is still in store for this earth. It will yet shine forth, this earth of ours. Or do you think that God will let His work go to the dogs, just because false men are fooling around on it? All this amounts to nothing. God's creation remains sublime. It will yet subject all spirits. The highest spirits in heaven and the lowest spirits in hell will yet have to submit to this earth when Jesus has His living church.

Can God reveal Himself in you, my friend? I will tell you when He can do it. It is when you are bent completely, fully, on God as love. Here the roads part. Believe me, I have rarely met a person who wanted this love of God. Does that surprise you? They all want to love, but they want to choose the people they love. They are cool toward or will even persecute with their hatred all those who do not suit them. Naturally everyone wants to love according to his sympathies. Everyone loves his family, his friends, his hobbies. However, it is quite a different matter to want God's love fully and completely. There is a love that rules in the name of man; it is the most dangerous thing in the world! The love of the members of one party judges people belonging to other parties.

The love of the members of one church loves only these and condemns all others. The love that is in the world tears God's love to pieces because it judges.

Yet there is a love which denies itself, which esteems all men as equals, which respects creation and no longer judges. There is a love which saves, which does away with evil and fights against all evil in order that the evil person may be saved. There is a love which does not want to do away with anybody, so that nothing may be lost, because Jesus is here, because God is the Father of all men. Remember this. Whoever does not want this love, which is God's love, will not recognize the living God, nor will he receive the revelation.

We recognize God's love when we see that the false man no longer counts for anything. We recognize the love of our God, the true God, in the coming of a love which raises us above evil desires, the cause of all conflict and strife. This love will no longer throw the world into wretchedness. So let us become free in our hearts. Something has already been given into man's hands. We have received sufficient light to break away. So make a beginning and no longer judge or condemn any man, just as Jesus has not condemned one single man. Fear every word that comes out of your false love. Be joyful and confident. Then you will recognize the Man who now sits at God's right hand in heaven. Make a beginning! Then there will be light on earth, and we shall know where the living church of Jesus is to be found on the earth.

May the Father in heaven have mercy on us! It

is our hope that the light may soon come. May God's kingdom unfold, not in the bustle of the world, not according to the desires of men who want to see all things judged, but according to the infinite love of God which separates good and evil, which redeems, illumines and sanctifies all things. Praised be the Father in our Lord Jesus Christ, in the Holy Spirit of God's love!

13
CHRIST IN THE FLESH

Today we want to open our hearts to the meaning of those mysterious, blessed words, **"God is revealed in the flesh."** The important thing for those who want to follow the Savior, Jesus Christ, is whether they can understand this mystery or not. Furthermore, there is the question whether in this understanding they retain the strength not only to say, "God is revealed in the flesh," but also to experience in reality that God is truly in the flesh.

We should not think that the matter is closed with the birth of the Savior. Nor should we imagine that because He died, rose again and ascended into heaven, it is now our duty to celebrate the birth of Jesus Christ. I believe that our risen Lord Jesus Christ does not care much whether we celebrate His birth, whether we immortalize the child in the manger or not. What matters to Him is not so much that we realize that He was once born. Rather He wants us to realize **that He is here.** He wants us to understand that this "God is in the flesh" has now become a truth, a world-wide truth, and that, in time, through the gospel it will become a truth in mankind.

"God is in the flesh" — this alone can raise humanity, and with it all flesh, the earth, the whole of creation, to a height which we have not yet attained. This lack causes much misery and death in our time. The apostle John once said, "Every man who does not acknowledge the coming of Jesus Christ in the flesh is not of God and does not belong to the living church of Jesus Christ." (1 John 4, 2; 2 John 7) By this he does not mean that we are to set up a creed and say, "Christ is the Son of God," and be done with it. Rather, he means that whoever in our day and in our church does not know that through the Lord Jesus Christ the almighty God is in our flesh, is not of God.

Already in the early times there were powers of opposition at work. They were caused by man's condition, full of sin, full of misery, full of death, full of unclarity. Looking at the peoples of that time, the Romans, the Greeks, the barbarians, the Egyptians, the Babylonians, one could think, "The Son of God may well have come into the flesh at one time; yet now He is in heaven. God cannot be in the flesh." Even many Christians were so greatly impressed by sin and death that they could no longer believe that God was in the flesh. They could no longer believe that Christ came into the flesh as the Word of God; that He was and remained in the flesh despite all sin and folly, despite all the confusion that has come over mankind. Christ **is** in the flesh. One denies this when one sees men just as they are, untouched by Christ; for it is true that in the flesh there also dwells something else — the flesh is filled with darkness.

I do not want to go into the intricate nature of this darkness. We know enough about all the evil it contains and about its effects. We know well that it leads to murder, theft and all manner of blasphemy. All I want to say is that the words "Christ in the flesh" are a signal for the battle against those other things which dwelled in the flesh before and still dwell in it. "Christ in the flesh" is the weapon against all that is in the flesh, whether you call it death, devil, Satan or darkness. Whatever you may call it, it is that part of us which each one desires to get rid of. There is some good in everyone, and we all feel, "I would like to be good, but I can't. I want to serve truth but am driven into deceit. I want to be just and am unjust. I do have the will, but I am unable to carry it through." Such feelings are in everyone's heart, and we all know of very sad experiences in our lives. Many condemn themselves because of this. Many have been told to fight this thing. Well, just try to fight it! For centuries men have studied, have invented ascetic practices and self-torture, to put an end to this thing. It has all been in vain. No man can wage this fight.

Yet the fight has been begun by the Spirit, who is in Christ. The Spirit fights; on Him we may rely. Christ in the flesh is the most powerful adversary of the devil in the flesh. Christ in the flesh opposes our injustice with God's justice. "Christ in the flesh" is the fight against sin, the fight of life against death.

This battle is truly being fought. It must continue; it must lead to victory.

In a sense, therefore, I would call it an illusion for Christians to seek peace, as though the gospel wanted to make life comfortable for them. The contrary is true; here the words apply, "I have not come to bring peace on earth, but a sword." As long as the fight is going on, we have peace only in the fight. Our peace is not well-being; it is not a placid quietude. Our peace is a participation in Christ, in God in the flesh against all the other things in the flesh. We should not console ourselves, either, with the fact that the Apostle said of himself, "I do have the will, but I am unable to carry it through." Many people then say, "So you see, we can't do anything; we can be saved only through grace." It is true. But we can become fighters through grace. Then we are redeemed!

Through grace we can go even into death. Through grace we need not give in, nor need we be discouraged by any situation of natural man. We need not think that we are necessarily miserable creatures who are never able to do any good at all. By grace we want to break through the laws of nature in us, for it is a deceitful nature. It is false man who lives in sin, in whom dwells sin. This is not man as God created him; it is a false man. Therefore the words "Christ in the flesh" mean that we should become true men again. They also mean believing in Jesus Christ, and knowing oneself to be a man of God at the side of the Lord Jesus. Then we can say to ourselves and to others, "It is not true that we belong to sin. What is in my flesh is not the true thing. Only when God dwells in my flesh am I a true man!"

In this struggle our fists, our intelligence and our understanding are of little use. All our efforts are almost in vain. Our faith alone can help us, the faith that **Jesus is victorious because He is in the flesh.** These words have often been understood to mean that Jesus triumphs and rules and comes in the end, on the last day of the world, like an apparition down from the blue. It will not help us if lights only come down to us from above. The light must shine within us now. The "above" of our Lord Jesus Christ is then within. It is within my heart, within your heart. It is wherever there is a fight for life or death, where people would rather give their last drop of blood than yield to sin. Not that I can get hold of sin and drive it out. Rather I say to sin, "Your end is prepared for you. It will come as surely as I live, because Jesus is in the flesh." Were He not in the flesh today, I would rather give up my faith. Then it would be an illusion. If I as flesh cannot have God fight in my flesh, then our cause is lost.

All flesh is of God: flowers and plants, animals, all that is created, is flesh. Something false can come into the whole created world, into everything we call physical life or flesh. We know this very well. Yet we say, "If Jesus is truly in the flesh, then finally all flesh must recognize God, even the plants and the animals, to say nothing of men. God shall rise, as the sun rises, out of the flesh of all peoples on the earth — Christ shall rise for the glory of God the Father.

In the black men this will come about according to their manner. We cannot incline them toward God. Christ in their black men's flesh must make men of God out of them, not by our standards but according to their own need. The same applies to the Chinese, the Japanese, the Hindus, or whoever they may be. "Christ in the flesh" are words which will fill us with love to all men, even to our enemies; they will dispose our hearts kindly toward the whole world. Not flattery for the world, but kindliness toward all men, is the higher friendship in which we maintain, in all situations, that Christ has come even into the flesh of sinners. It is but a question of time until the other things will have gone out of them so that Jesus may live.

This, my friends, is the meaning of Christ's day, of Christmas, if we want to celebrate such a day. I wish the usual kind of celebrations would stop, so that each day might become Christ's day. Then through our faith each day could spread a light of Christ which would really be visible. Then people would see that Christ is truly in the flesh, in our human society. Our human society must spread a divine light in honor of God the Father. We want to become aware of this. We want to fight for it by recognizing that Christ came into the flesh and with Him, God.

Here and now Christ begins this fight. He does not wrestle with men; He does not wrestle with a single man. He does not snatch up one man and throw him into hell, and then another and throw him into heaven. Never, as long as there has been Christianity, have we seen Jesus Christ do this. Only those who seek their piety elsewhere than with God, do this. They condemn people right and left, and in the middle they select a few that please them and pronounce them as saved. Jesus has never yet had a part in such things; these were brought in by pious people in all centuries. Jesus does not start wrestling with the flesh. He starts a fight in the flesh, a fight with darkness, with sin in you. He does not pick a quarrel with you; He does not want to deal with you in a rage in order that you may overcome sin in yourself. Christ did not come to be our teacher in the world, or our tyrant. He came to be our redeemer. He came to overcome in our flesh all that is not of God. This must be cast out because Christ is in the flesh.

But in individuals the victory will not be perfect until the whole of mankind is able to experience it. Thus all our striving and struggling, even that of the best of Jesus' disciples, of the apostles, is not yet perfect. Nobody, not even an apostle, can say, "Now I am through; now I can help others." Even in the apostles and in the best of the disciples the fight goes on. Individual man represents the fight which has to be waged in the whole world. Therefore we must not despair if we individuals have not achieved clarity so quickly. We must only have the certainty that full clarity will come, that it must come, because Jesus is in the flesh.

Let the whole world come and kill us; I shall not defend myself. Let all the devils come, let all the angels of darkness come, let all darknesses come — here I stand; I do not will to defend myself, I need not defend myself. Why? Because I know that Christ is in the flesh. Should I have fear and say, "I am a sinner"? No! For then Christ would not be in the flesh. If I have to fear my own sin, then Christ did not come into the flesh. I need fear no sin, no death. If Christ came into this flesh in which sin and death dwell, then I am free! Even though I am still a sinner, I am free. The victory is on my side, on your side. Only believe it, carry it in your hearts, change your lives, then you are converted. Nothing else is needed. You need not appear to be better men now. If a man lives in the knowledge and experience that Jesus is now in the flesh, then everything else will come by itself. Even if many people do not yet feel it, sooner or later the light will dawn in them too, because Jesus is in the flesh. If you believe this, you are converted.

This is the kind of conversion I would like to see in our house. I don't care for any other kind of piety. None of our own efforts to organize life and to set up rules and regulations have any value for me. There is only one thing I want, that in the midst of the suffering and misery, of labor and temptation, in life and in death, you may be able to say, "Christ is in the flesh! What can separate us from the love of God?" I wish that you, who live in this house with me, could all say this together wholeheartedly.

Of course we shall have to go through many experiences. We cannot deny that we have many experiences, including bitter ones. It is not a very pleasant matter to accept fully the words "Christ in the flesh," to say wholeheartedly, "I count everything as loss, that I may gain Christ." (Phil. 3, 8) Most Christians don't like this; they want to see their own interests taken care of first. But, whether it will bring peace or conflict, understanding or misunderstanding, this remains the truth: Christ is God in the flesh.

We may be certain that we are created of God. According to His will we are born anew and created anew. We are all different and none of us is yet perfect; but we stand in a movement toward a new heaven and a new earth. Therefore, my friends, we want to retain this certainty in the awareness of victory not only today but every day and in future times. In joy and confidence we know that God is revealed in the flesh. Let us exalt our Lord in the flesh, Jesus Christ. Let us hold high the banner and never let it fall. Though it may be a fight unto death, let us never lose heart, never lose courage, never give way to sin, never take the side of darkness! Nothing has any power, nothing has any authority, other than this Christ in the flesh to whose glory we sang already 56 years ago:

> Jesus is victorious King,
> Who o'er all his foes has conquered.
> Jesus, soon the world will fall
> At His feet, by love o'erpowered.
> Jesus leads us with His might
> From the darkness to radiant light.

14

I AM THE LORD

I am the Lord, and there is no other. I form light and create darkness, I make weal and create woe, I am the Lord, who do all these things.
—Isaiah 45, 6-7

We all know that we men stand between light and darkness. It is no secret to anyone, not even to the gentiles. Everyone knows, too, that in light there is life and in darkness there is death. It is equally known to all that in life there is good and in death there is evil, and that this duality brings us into terrible need. This is actually the mystery of our earthly life. The greatest minds have been puzzling ever since ancient times over how to solve this mystery.

Why is this? It is because few know God, who is above light and darkness. God is one. As soon as there is another beside Him, there is darkness. He is the only good one, and as soon as something rules beside Him it becomes evil by this very fact. Thus God is also the reason why evil must be evil and darkness must be dark, because it separated itself from Him. It would be a sad thing if it were not so, if darkness could also be good, if something that is outside of God could also be light. This would not be right. That is the good thing about creation, that we can say, "All good gifts, all perfect gifts come from above, from the Father of light, in whom there is no darkness." Darkness is outside of Him, not in Him. He is all goodness in himself. All good things in creation come from Him. Therefore all things that cannot be brought into connection with Him must be called darkness. Because of Him they must be called darkness and appear as darkness. Because of Him they must be called evil. All things that exist outside of Him must become evil by that very fact.

This is a great comfort for us. Now we know that even the darkness is utterly dependent on Him, that evil cannot escape His hand. It cannot exist independently. God, and no one else, caused darkness to come upon evil and death to come upon sin. Therefore we know that the world, the whole world, is in God's hands.

There is no such thing as two worlds, one in God's hands and the other one not. There are not two species of man, one under God's rule and the other completely outside of God's will. No! For even where things are quite dark, God alone is the Lord. No devil can do what he wants, no wicked angel can achieve anything. Satan is in darkness because of God. There he lives his own kind of life which unfortunately is contagious and deadly to those who are attracted by it. Yet the entire realm of sinfulness and deadliness is and remains God's realm, firmly held in His hands. Let us carry this knowledge in our hearts as a witness. I would like to say to every devil, "Your Satan is under God. You cannot make a single move. You cannot move one finger. You are under God!"

Unless we know this, we cannot understand how Christ came into the world. **Into the world** — the good one? Into the evil world! **Into the flesh** — the good flesh? Into the evil flesh! It is wonderful to think that God loved the world. Which world? The world that became diabolical, the godless world! The people who lived in darkness saw a great light. The desperate, the condemned, the damned, the murdered, the miserable, all those for whom there was no longer any consolation, no longer any hope, were allowed to see the Father. To them it is given to see the Father, who loves them. Before that there was only darkness, there was evil, though it was in God's hands. Now there is light; at least the light is possible.

The light was promised. It was called into the darkness of death. This light becomes love. The gospel becomes God's love in the darkness. With every word of the gospel proclaimed by Jesus or by His disciples in His name, God lays claim to the darkness, a loving claim, that is. Before, one could have felt that they were in God's hands; but alas, it is terrible to fall into the hands of the living God! Now we need no longer fear; for God lays claim to sin, death and hell through His love. He loves you, His child. "What, His child?" Perhaps you are a terrible sinner and God says to you, "I lay claim to you not just to judge and condemn you, but to help you." This you must know so that you can believe. This is the gospel, to tell people, to tell sinners, to tell the whole world, "God lays His hand upon you, not to destroy you, but to help you. Therefore accept this help. Thus you will know that God is **your Father.**"

This should be our message. However, before we can proclaim it, it must take root in our own hearts.

We must first know God before we are able to proclaim the gospel. I know of few people who have the gospel in their hearts. They are all Christians, but they do not have the gospel in their hearts. They are all a little bit evil. Try as one may, one cannot make the gospel enter into people's hearts. Yet one must not give up, though one is often weary. I have to confess that this is what makes me tired. Or should I be content with people who have nothing but hatred? Should I be content with people who do not understand God's love? People who have more respect for the devil than for God? Who fear darkness more than they fear God? Should I be content with people who are more afraid of sin than of God, and who tremble at the idea of death more than they fear God? I cannot be content with such people, for they do not have the gospel in their hearts. This is why they are not a light in the world.

There may be many Christians all over the place, and yet no one feels that the light is here, that it is Christ's light! The Christians are not the light. The gospel is the light. You must have the gospel in your heart; it must come from God, "who makes the light and creates the darkness." God, who in Christ lays claim to all men, will enable you to give a witness and to tell everybody, to think of everybody, that he is God's. Even if he were a devil, he is God's. No other power, no ruler, no one, in heaven or on the earth or beneath the earth, can move one finger. Our God alone is Lord over all that lives. They will yet have to bend their knees, all of them, whether they want to or not. They will all have to acknowledge that there is none beside Him!

These things must live in our hearts as a witness. No man, no spirit, is allowed to pretend that he too can achieve something. Some people are so proud as to think they too can do something. Many authorities are built up on earth, apparent powers, human currents; these are the strongest forces. Even Christianity has often yielded to such human currents, saying, "What can one do? One has to give in to people!" These are the strongest authorities on earth. There are German, English, European, Asiatic currents, party currents, social currents. A whole mass of people is caught up by them. They sweep everything else along with them. If you refuse to go along with the stream they hate you. Then there is hostility, discord, bloodshed, a hateful life.

These things seem to have an enormous power. If, for instance, such a current of unbelief suddenly seizes mankind and ignores God, it seems to be terribly powerful. It isn't really so very powerful. But it is distressing when the very people on whom the cause really ought to depend — because they say they believe in God — don't really quite trust Him. Still they are afraid of those authorities and principalities. Still they give in and succumb to the human custom of saying, "What else can one do?" Then it seems as though God were not really the Lord, as though there were a devil who is master, and that is a lie. We have never yet put faith in the devil. Therefore we said already 55 years ago, "Jesus alone is victor!" There is no master, not even in the darkness, who does not have to yield to our Lord! There is but one Lord, there is but one God. Nothing else is master, nor has it any power. Nothing else has any right or any claim for itself. No hell, no death or devil can make any claim. All things are God's.

If we men take this stand, then darkness must go. This is the stand you must take in yourself too; then the darkness in you has to vanish. You are tormented, distressed, insulted, because the darkness hurts you. Give up your respect and your fear of the darkness — fear God! Then perhaps darkness may still plague you outwardly, but there will be a fight, and as a fighter you will be protected by the hand of God. Fear nothing but God! Do not say that anyone else is the master, has power, has authority. This is false, wrong, nothing but lies and deception. One alone is the Lord! In your sorrow, in your sickness, in your temptation, in all that wants to torment you, in your sin, one alone is the Lord! All things are placed under this one who loves you and wants to help you. This we must believe if we want to solve the mystery of the world.

We must drive the darkness out. How can we do that? Perhaps by saying, "Such and such people belong to the devil, to death"? That is no way to do it. We should stand up wherever we are, saying, "Away with you, darkness, sin, death! You have no business here. And if you were to get hold of all men, still you would have to give them back, each one of them!" This is the way to drive the darkness out. Therefore the Savior demands of us that we love even our enemies. He will not tolerate that we hate or condemn our enemies. It is extremely important to Him that we not be judges in the world, that we think of no one as not belonging to God. Even when it goes against our feelings, when we see the worst of men, we must still be able to think, "It is merely a question of time. In any case he is God's already today, even though he is in darkness. The darkness is under God too." We drive it away first from ourselves, who believe in Jesus Christ. In the firm knowledge of victory we may then oppose the darkness and say, "You belong to God! You must be subject to Him!"

If we take this stand, then we shall experience eternal life in our own lives. Then we shall experience all manner of good things coming from God to ourselves and to other people. Many times I have thought and said, "I am firmly convinced that in our time God comes closer." There must have been people who did not admit the darkness, who have said, "Jesus alone is the Lord." They must have declared without wavering, in all situations, "Jesus alone is the Lord. The whole earth belongs to the Lord!" Only in this way can I explain the many good things which have come to us from above even in our time. At the present time the whole European world is talking of peace, although they don't have it yet. Why do they talk about it? Who can explain this? Since the dawn of mankind no one has ever spoken about peace. Today they talk about the hope that the nations might consider whether they could not get along without war. Such a thing was impossible in all the past centuries.

So here we do have something good; here a part of the darkness has been driven out.

There are many other things in our days of which one could say that they are good. There is all manner of life, of love, of hope, and of health, in contrast with other times. Much good is coming into the world nowadays. Of course men don't know where it comes from; so they complain about our present time. They say the times are bad, because they don't believe in anything. Never mind whether they believe or not; they will yet have to acknowledge that God is God. As long as there are a few amongst them who carry God's love in their hearts and believe in the gospel, the darkness will be driven out of the whole world. Then good will come, peace will come, and the light of life will shine into death itself.

This is the calling of Jesus' disciples. Of them the Savior says that He wants to give them the kingdom. What does that mean? The Savior will give the kingdom to a disciple — maybe to you, maybe to me — to one who believes in Him. He will give it to one who believes in the Lord, in Him who is Lord over all things. He will give it to one who does not admit any prince of darkness, but who says at all times, "Jesus is the Lord!" To such a disciple He will give the right to say on earth, "Away with you, darkness; away with you, evil. Away with all that does not want to submit to God's hand and to the rulership of the Lord Jesus."

This is our calling. If we suffer with Him, we shall also rule with Him. Surely there is enough suffering. If we place ourselves at the side of the Savior, then there will be much suffering. Manifold are Christ's sufferings; but we rejoice in them, we are glad. This is the fight. If we suffer with Him, we shall rule with Him. We, who believe in the Savior, shall rule. Of course this does not mean to go over other people's heads, to judge men, to beat up servants, to be angry and annoyed at those we dislike. No! It means to rule in the way Jesus rules. It means to rule in the love of the Father. It means to say, "In the name of Jesus Christ I say to you, darkness, you must be destroyed. You sin, you serpent, you Prince of death, you must perish. You are nothing to us!" This is what it means to rule.

We are allowed to take this into our hands just because it is a fact that our God holds all things in His hands; because there are not two kingdoms, a kingdom of darkness and a kingdom of God. There is but one kingdom, God's kingdom. True, in this one kingdom there is yet darkness over all those who are still in sin; but it is one kingdom. There may be two rooms in a house, but it is one house, not two. All things are in one, in our God. Therefore, if we are in this house of our God, we may rule in the darkness, in sin, in death. We must not weaken, nor must we think that we cannot carry on. We can always go on. The victory is ours again and again. Finally the complete victory must penetrate the whole of creation. God must be God on the earth as in heaven, and beneath the earth, and wherever His creatures are.

Let this live in our hearts. This is so necessary in

our days, when we feel more than ever God's rulership. Especially today it is necessary for people to understand this. Please, I ask you, please don't grumble so much about the world! Those who grumble about the world are not living in the love of the Father. Neither should you condemn the godless, the unbelievers, the strangers, the dark! That is not our business. It is not for us to condemn, not for us to judge. Only witness to the truth that God is God and none other! Carry in your hearts the gospel of the loving Father. In Jesus He gives to all flesh the hope of eternal life. Then you will also find peace in your personal struggles. Then you will be allowed to experience the victory of the Savior in your own lives. Then you will be allowed to take your part in preparing the way for the kingdom of God which will come over all nations on the earth.

15

JESUS AMONG THE WRETCHED

> For man believes with his heart and so is justified, and he confesses with his lips and so is saved.
> —Romans 10, 10

By these words the Apostle Paul wants to prepare a way for the Lord Jesus; for in Him a new light rises over all life, a light that stands in contrast to the old world which is under the law. Now there is to be a man, a Lord, a God, on the earth; for Him the way must be prepared. We repeat Paul's words because we want to prepare the way for the Savior. In speaking them, we think of the fact that Jesus Christ will come into the midst of our own lives. For we know of no spirit in heaven or on the earth that is greater than He. We know of nothing that ever happened in the history of man that is greater than the coming of Jesus. We know of no revelation and of no grace which could be greater than that which Jesus Christ wants to be on earth. The important thing, however, is to give Jesus the honor due Him, and that is not an easy matter.

After Jesus had died and ascended into heaven, He was no longer in people's thoughts. Already in the times of the apostles, many were about to forget Him. Of course, He couldn't be forgotten in the sense that no one ever thought of Him at all. He had penetrated so deeply into the history of men that He could not really be forgotten. But what He **wants,** what is to come through Him on earth — this can be forgotten.

The disciples and followers of Jesus must fight and give their whole hearts to prepare the way for Him. In this they must see their justification. They are to prepare the way so that what is to happen on earth through this Son of God really will happen. Let us give our whole hearts to this; this is our justification. Let us give our whole voice for this; this is our salvation. Of course I don't mean just the voice; I would rather say, let us give our deeds. For unless I do that to which I confess with my voice, it is worthless. So then let us give our whole hearts and our whole doing, our whole energy, that Jesus may come into His own. That is the calling of those who follow Jesus, then and now.

Who is Jesus, then? This question almost brings us into difficulties, for in a way we have to place ourselves in opposition to the historical development of Christianity. A large Christianity has developed around the name of Jesus Christ, but the minds of Christians have become too otherworldly, so to speak. Their longing for Jesus, their adoration of Jesus Christ, has become too otherworldly. In their hearts and in their deeds, men hold on to Him and hope for Him in a spiritual way only. In the realm of the spiritual they formulate a certain confession to Him, and so the Christian religions came about. These could never have been the goal that Jesus wanted, for these Christian religions give us no faith and no insight. Everywhere there are different kinds of belief; at times these beliefs are modified. This can never have been God's will in Jesus.

God's will in Jesus becomes visible in Jesus' life on earth. Who is He? He is the friend of men, of human society. In His characteristic manner He takes hold of human society by its lowest part. With a strong hand Jesus takes hold of the miserable, the despised, the little people, the masses. Now everything rushes in on Him; people call Him a blasphemer and a servant of sin. They say that He is a man to be rejected and despised; nevertheless He steps in firmly where no one ever ventured before Him. Thus the miserable come to the light for the first time, and so do the sick, those whose spirits are confused, the whole mass of people for whom human society has no use. Jesus steps in amongst the despised, the enslaved, those who are looked down upon. He comes to the people who are ignored by those intellectuals who have created an abyss between educated and uneducated, between rich and poor, between high and low. Jesus intervenes on the level of those who are ignored by the history of the nations and of society. These miserable people who have never come to the light are the very ones whose side Jesus takes. The sick must come out, the mentally deranged must come to the light, the poor must come to the surface. The despised, the enslaved, the imprisoned, the rejected, those who are slighted by the educated people, all these must come to the surface.

Jesus is much more substantially "man" than any human being ever was. This fact bears witness that He is the Son of God. Any other, who has not come from God, cannot take up the cause of this class of people to this very day. No one who cares only about education will go to such people. A man who lives only for philosophy and science, a man who has only human love and human mercy — in other words, a man of the kind we find nowadays, will not go to such people. He will always think, "Oh well, that isn't so important." But if he meets a gentleman, a person who is honored and respected, he will think, "I must stick to this one." Anyone who wants to found a new party, anyone who wants to amount to anything in the world, seeks his friends in the higher regions of human society. These lofty spirits, these highest of all angels, are incapable of doing what Jesus can do. They cannot take up the cause of these miserable people.

Many different spiritual directions are coming into fashion these days. People are studying right and left; they soar to intellectual heights; they compose theosophical images; they study philosophy. Yet not a single one of all these great minds enters where Jesus entered. Such is the greatness of the Savior. Where Jesus entered, there the renewal of human society is to begin. This sounds rather strange, for we are used to setting our hopes on lofty minds. We set our hopes on the highest regions of heaven, while Jesus sets His hopes on the poor, on the outcasts, on those who are rejected by kings and emperors. His hopes are with those who are a mere plaything in the hands of rulers. Here it is that Jesus sees the beginning of renewal.

Do we want to follow Jesus on this way? Then we must accept Him in this company. Then the call comes to us to set to work wholeheartedly, for **here** is Jesus. He himself, speaking about the time of His absence, does not say, "I was rich and you respected me." He says, "I was poor, I was hungry, I was thirsty, I was imprisoned, and you came to me, to the poor Savior. You came to me, who sat as a guest at the table of the lowest of men. There you came to me." Here must be your whole heart; here you must do the deeds of faith; for it is from here that the power comes which will overthrow the world, the wretched, **unhappy world.**

People are afraid of the collapse of the world. I am looking forward to it. I wish it would begin right now to crash and break apart. For this world of the humanly great is and remains the cause of all misery. They cannot do anything about it, these well-intentioned people, these good kings and ministers, these excellent prelates and popes. However much they try, they cannot. I would like to tell all of them, "You **cannot** do it!" Many times one hopes and thinks that there is one who has achieved something. One praises some action, one hopes for success and thinks, "Now it comes." And yet only a little later one realizes that one was again deceived; afterwards it is worse than before.

True, men do achieve quite a lot on the surface. They help a little to prevent the miserable from drowning altogether. They educate the minds of some, but only at the cost of oppressing others. This is a terrible curse that comes limping along behind our civilization and always keeps up with us in spite of its limp. We are incapable of building up a civilization without killing people. Men are constantly being sacrificed, human beings are killed, because of our civilization. I have often spoken of the pain I feel when riding in a train or using any of the conveniences which we enjoy nowadays. So many have to sweat and toil, to live a life of care and misery, in order that we may enjoy the comforts and advantages of modern civilization! Everything we do is done at the cost of others. Our whole life drives others into death. In the end blood is the fruit of the earth.

However, it shall not remain like this. Jesus is the true man, the true representative of human society. Yet how difficult it is for this Jesus to live among us! Who believes in Him? Who wants His justice? Who wants to turn to the sinners? For now we are not only told to believe in Jesus. We are also told to have faith for the sinners, for the depraved, for the miserable, for the murdered ones, for those who are not alive. **This is Jesus.**

If it were only a matter of worshipping the Lord Jesus all by himself in His elevation, it would be an easy thing for people to do. They love it, they like to fall down before Him. They find it easy to worship any statue made of gold and silver. But Jesus does not want to be worshipped in this way. He does not want to be adored as something separate from men. He wants to be worshipped in connection with the sinners.

This was too hard already for the Pharisees at the time. At the time of the apostles it was too hard for the new Christians among the Jews. They could not understand that Jesus was to be worshipped among the gentiles, that He was to be seen with the despised, that He was to be sought among these. This was terribly hard for them. The apostles spent themselves in the fight and were hardly able to hold out. The whole New Testament echoes the struggle of the spirits against **this** Jesus. At first there were the proud Jews who looked down upon the Gentiles from the heights of their religious tradition. Later, after the apostles had died and could no longer speak, heathen philosophy found its way into the Christian church. Then the Christian sages, the great Christian minds, the Christian rulers, took things into their own hands and fought against this "Jesus among the persecuted."

Not even the Christian church was able to resist this. Like the heathens, the Christians persecuted millions of people. Anyone who, in their eyes, did not appear immediately as a just man was damned. It is unfortunate that to this very day we find not one single Christian confession that would not say, "We condemn, we condemn." They can't help it; the human element in them is too strong. Something in them resists this Jesus to the utmost.

Later too, during the time of the Reformation, there was extreme persecution and killing. Anything that could not immediately reach the high regions of one of the Reformers and great minds was beaten down. All that remained, so to speak, on the ground, all that lay prostrate and crippled, was trodden underfoot. Anyone who had ideas other than those pleasing to the leading spirits, was crushed. Everything had to conform to the will of the kings, the princes, the mighty.

I wish, my friends, that you too could feel my grief over this "Jesus amongst the sinners." Unless we grieve, we cannot come fully to this Jesus. No one who lives partly under an illusion can fight for this Jesus. No one who thinks that with this refined Christianity and with this "believing from above" he can achieve anything in the true spirit of Jesus, will find Him. First a light must dawn in us that makes us see how violent the fight is. The fight for this Jesus is a fight unto death. It is a fight which is opposed to our entire nature, to all our experiences. I could tell you much of my efforts, of how I tried to help people in their misery. Hundreds of times I was fooled and deceived. Many times my ears rang with the words, "You are a fool! Stick to the educated people, the good people, the right kind of people, stick to those who are in the know. At least one can rely on them."

But no! These are devilish voices. No, I say to them, a thousand times no! I want to fight for the sinners, for the miserable, for the despised, until my last breath. It would be my greatest joy if I were able to show to all those who live in such heights how much rottenness there is among them. Even in my own house I would like to call out every day, "Keep to the lowly!" All too often we look like a very distinguished company. You should be ashamed of being so refined! I wish to God that the refined, distinguished people had to withdraw into the corners, and the place were full of ragamuffins. We would be a hundred times happier if we proclaimed this Jesus.

The ragged and poor will yet come! They have been misled, scared away, deceived. They no longer have any confidence in us. They think that we want to have nothing to do with them. They think we despise them and can't stand them. They think we are ashamed of them. So we must get along without them. Sometimes we can meet them in church. They sit around in the churches, but they don't really belong to us. We are not filled with a faith in the justice which Jesus brings to the sinners. We are not filled with the justice which Jesus sets up in the very place where the proud cannot enter. Yet this is precisely where something must begin to happen. If we think about it, we shall understand with our minds that only out of the large, uneducated masses can the true help for the world come. Only through them can the renewal come which will truly set mankind on a different path. This cannot possibly come from single, highly cultivated minds. It can come only from amongst those with whom Jesus walks. To these Jesus asks the Father to send His Spirit.

No doubt someone could come and say, "Jesus never came into the world for anything like this. He does not want to change the world. He just wants those who know of Him to be saved after their death. He never wanted anything else. This is what has been believed for 1900 years. What you are trying to say about Jesus is something He never wanted."

It would be no use entering into a discussion. All I can say is: Behold the Jesus who was born in Bethlehem, the one who proclaimed the gospel to the poor. Behold the Jesus who comes to all the wretched and sick and helps them, the one who feeds the crowds in the desert. Behold the Jesus who sees the common people, those who have no shepherd, those whom He wants to draw unto himself when He is raised up. Behold this Jesus! Then the light will dawn in you. He really wants to achieve something on earth. What good is it if a few people are saved? On all the earth a new light must shine.

Here, in our human society, things must change. Here dwells the real Satan who has to be overcome. The earth in itself is beautiful, the sky is beautiful. Everything God has created is beautiful and good, but we men have lost the connection between ourselves and the creation which surrounds us. We have lost our bearings as to the real task we have on earth. We do not even know properly how to get along with our own folks. Parents don't know how to live with their children; brothers and sisters don't know how to live with each other; neighbors don't know how to get along with one another. There is a tremendous confusion in us men.

We must protest against this confusion, so that the truth of life may come to light. We must fight against this lie which is in us, against this sin, this world sin which causes our separation from the truth. If we fight against this world sin, then a light will dawn in us and we will understand this Jesus of the common people, this Savior of men. Then we shall be able to understand that the whole world must look to Him, for He is the only one who pursues this goal. Other spirits pursue other goals. Leave them to it. Jesus wants to build up a human society in God's praise and honor, **here on earth.** His great goal is that the nations may yet come to Zion and worship. He wants the whole world to behold the glory of their God.

So let us believe with our whole hearts, let us confess with all our strength, that Jesus is the Lord. Let us believe and confess it in such a way that we are at all times with the lowly and the despised. Let us seek the Savior amongst these, and not only in the heavens above. The heaven of Jesus Christ will be among the despised, among the outcasts. Here we want to seek Him, here shall our hearts be. Let us reach out to these with all our energy. Then we shall see how great a power this Jesus is.

Let me tell you, if we were able to gather a group of people for this Jesus, the world would marvel at the light which would shine forth from them. A light would shine in the very midst of our deadly nature, of our misery, our poverty, our helplessness. Then there would soon be an end to social and political problems; the confusion would come to an end. Such a living church, gathered around this Jesus, radiates freedom, abundant life and love. From it the spirit of truth and power shines forth, and its light surpasses everything that mankind has seen until then. May God grant that men recognize this Jesus, that they believe in Him. May God grant that men confess to **this Jesus!**

16
"I AM WITH YOU!"

Behold, I am with you all through the days that are coming, until the consummation of the world!
—Matthew 28, 20 (Knox)

"I am with you!" These words should fill our hearts, for they are the greatest truth which can be given to us. As time goes by we may be inclined to become weak and discouraged by the fleeting nature of all that surrounds us. We truly do not know from one day to the next whether even the most precious thing will remain with us. It is then that the great God himself will step in among us. Also in earlier times He has appeared among men. "I am your shield, your great reward." — "I will bless you." — "I am the God who will never forsake you." — "Even if I am angry with you, I will also be compassionate, as a mother has compassion for her child."

Thus the voice of God was heard in ancient times, in the midst of the dark and fleeting world of mankind. Individual men were given new life and new strength in this presence of God. Such was the strength they found in it that to this day their witness and their lives are a joy and a comfort to us. Now it comes to us also, quite simply and humanly, in the words, "I am with you." The Savior, born as one of us, but from the heavenly heights says to us, "I am the light of the world." — "I am meek and lowly of heart." — "I will refresh you." — "I will not let you become orphans." — "I am with you all through the days, until the end of the world."

This presence of God, my friends, is our religion. In it we must live. God is among us, He is close to us, and we may rejoice in Him. We are not alone with our own self; God himself steps into our midst. No greater truth can be written into our hearts.

At the beginning of a new year each one considers his own life; how is it with him? How weak, how poor, how foolish, how sinful and how utterly lost we feel! How dark and troubled our fate often appears to us! We are hardly able to see ahead. There is very little we can provide for, very little we can do. We have to doubt everything we do, for we don't know what will come of it. But all things will change; all things will become new. "I make all things new. I will make you new in your poverty, in your pain, in your doubts, in your sins. In all things I will make you new, poor man that you are. I will make you so new that you will no longer be poor, that you need no longer grieve, that you need no longer despair of yourself. For you are no longer alone. Something new fills you, the presence of the Savior who has bound you to himself." A power will be with us which will give us the strength to triumph in our lives.

In the life of every human being there is a struggle unto death, a painful fight, and the eternal question, "How will it go with me? How shall I bear it all?" Each single human being is like a troubled world, full of storms and attacks, of deep pain and death pangs. Many times one is hardly able to draw a breath. Yet now rejoice — the victory will be yours! When the Lord Jesus says, "Behold I make all things new, and I am with you," then you need no longer be concerned for your own soul, your own life, your eternal life. Your fight will be a daily victory.

Another very special significance lies in Christ's words; for by them the Savior allows us to see the world through His own eyes. Mankind as a whole is like an individual struggling in darkness and surrounded by night. It fights and labors for a better fate, for a new world of justice. It struggles painfully for a world in which the true divine image of man may become clearly visible everywhere. We cannot separate ourselves from the many to whom the great, redeeming nature of God is not yet revealed. There is a power which drives us into faraway lands, to the strangest peoples. This same power drives us also here at home down into the darkest company, into the most degenerate areas of human life. My friends, it is our task to long for the presence of the Savior to enter into those places. We must, if possible, carry it where it is darkest, where hope has almost been given up, where ruin and corruption stare back at us and take away our breath.

Shall we lose courage? No! For we know, we really know, the greatness of God's presence. We know who Jesus Christ is, the one who says, "I give my life for the world." We know the great expanse of the realm out of which the voice of God, the voice of Jesus Christ, speaks to us. This is a mighty domain, full of strength and victory. Here the Lord Jesus is surrounded by manifold powers. In the same way we may find ourselves surrounded by great, powerful hosts, and the victory of our Savior can be fully revealed to us.

Whenever we hear the words, "I am with you," we should be filled with a sensation of the endless power and might that lie in the hands of the Savior. For He came from God. He is the true Son of God. He makes us God's children. He is the victory over this human world, whose flesh He has taken on. He is the comfort for the corrupted. He is the life of the dying and of the dead. He is in heaven and on the earth and beneath the earth. In every abyss, in all depths, in all darknesses, in all alien territories, He is the great power of God which will transform all things. Of Him it shall be said in the end, "Truly, He has made all things new."

Let this word of God be your strength! Let it be your watchword for the New Year. Let not your own gifts, your own powers, your own human abilities, be your strength. Rather, let the voice of God be your strength, the voice that says to you, "I am with you all the days." If we live completely and fully in this presence, its power will be felt by our fellowmen as well as in our own lives. In this way we shall be messengers of the gospel on earth. We shall proclaim it with our whole being, and no longer with words, with human thoughts or with outward forms and force. This gospel has God's power to save all those who have open ears for it.

Never doubt, for Jesus says, "Through all the days." What are days? We often feel so lonely, our days are so dark, that at times we cannot even think of the presence of God. At other times we are so very foolish, and later we realize how many foolish things we have done. This fills us with disquiet, pain and repentance, to the point where we would like to do away with ourselves. Yet even the darkest days are your days; remember this! They belong to your days; at the end of your earthly life every day that you have lived belongs to your days. All these years, these hours, these times that you spend, are yours. All your experiences, all your joys, all that gives you courage for life, all that tries to depress you, to sadden you — all this belongs to your days. Into these days, which are yours, enters the Savior himself. Do not think that a single day passes when the Lord Jesus does not stand behind you. Perhaps you are so deep in darkness and night that you do not notice it at all. Yet He says, "I am with you through all your days! All your days are in my hand! If they are soiled, I shall cleanse them. If they become dark, I shall allow light to appear in your darkness, so that you may again feel joy. If they are happy days, then look, I am also there. Never forget it; believe in these words and live with them: I am with you through all your days."

When you look back over your life you may recall many days of which you are ashamed. Yet you must believe! If even now you are moved by God's Spirit and repent, then surely Jesus was also present in the days when you did not know Him yet. From the hour when you learn to know Him, He penetrates with His meekness and humility, with His life and death, into all your days, down into the first day of your life. Backwards into all your days the redeeming Spirit of Jesus pierces, backwards where so much in you was wrong. Thus you may be comforted even in your past. Thus you may say about your past, "Even then God was with me." He reaches down into all our days so deeply that our own life is illumined by His presence. Now we may indeed become God's representatives among men.

My friends, let us grasp this fully and deeply. Then the Savior will be able to say to us too, "You are the light of the world; you are the salt of the earth." Can you understand this, poor human being that you are? Can you understand that you too may become a person born not of men, but of God? Can you grasp that even in your poor human body you may represent the Savior? For this is how it should be, my friends. Wherever we are, whatever we do, our own person must represent the Savior. Therefore take good care to be silent often, so that your true self may speak. Do not be too quick to act according to your own nature. Always remember that your voice is now the Savior's voice. You have a great task. All your fighting and living, your pain and your victories, must now witness to the Savior. For truly, if we are comforted, then the whole world is comforted. If we have forgiveness of sins, then the whole world must have it. If we triumph over death and suffering, then let it be the Savior who speaks to other people out of our death and suffering and says, "Be comforted; I shall not leave you!" Thus all that we live, in all our days, will become a powerful gospel.

Many people think that goodness alone can proclaim God. No! No, indeed! Unless we ourselves are saved again and again from fear and suffering, we are nothing to the world. We Christians are no good at all unless we are born anew from God, brought back to life from death. Unless we go through suffering and sorrow because Jesus is with us, unless in Him we can overcome all afflictions however deep they may be, we shall be no good in the world. Therefore Christ's suffering continues through our own days.

We shall still have to suffer; we shall still have to bear heavy burdens. Yet I have great hopes for the times which are now to come. I hope for a great liberation, indeed for the greatest redemption.

Somewhere, however, somewhere and in some person, the darkness, the suffering, the chains and fetters that bind men, must be broken down. Maybe you are to be the bound one, so that your bonds may be loosed. Maybe you are to be the sad one, so that in you the comfort can be given. Maybe you are to be the dying one, so that in you the resurrection of Jesus Christ can become revealed. For all these things must happen in a personal way. God himself steps in among us personally; Jesus Christ is with us quite personally. We may rejoice to know that He, who is so great, binds himself to us in His very person. Therefore we should also see everything we do quite personally as a service to God in the world.

So let us not be afraid! Let us always remember that whatever we have to overcome is important also for others. If we know the Savior, if the Lord Jesus is with us, then through us the powers must be shown which shall dwell on earth amongst men. Not that we Christians should make ourselves at home and become great on earth; rather, the Lord Jesus shall be at home among us. God's being, our Father, shall be at home among us. The presence of the Savior in us and among us should be our greatest joy. Let us stand together, believe together, be joyful together, so firmly that we become one house. Into this house the Lord Jesus will gladly enter and say, "I come to you gladly, for you know that I must make all things, that I must create all things. You know that it is my death and my resurrection alone which can help the world."

A new time will begin, my friends, once the Lord Jesus has truly made His dwelling on earth. We must step back and become His servants. Then whatever we do will bear the stamp of His work. Then the new time will begin. In past years there have been too many Christians — some have even used violence — and too little of Christ. Yet Christ is the salvation of the world. The Savior must come!

The Lord Jesus binds us to the end of the world through His presence. The present time with all its pain and sin and corruption is to have an end. The Lord Jesus will be with us until the end of this world of death, this world of sin, this world of folly. He will be with us until the end of this world which causes so much heartbreak. Thus the Lord Jesus binds us to this end. We are allowed to look toward it. All that is evil, corrupt and sinful will have an end. Are you afraid? Are you afraid of the power of sin? Are you afraid of the power of death? No! A thousand times no! No! No! There will be an end.

Everything that is not of God will come to an end. The world, the human world, will have an end. It will not remain forever as we now see it. Thanks be to God that even now, in small things, an end is given. My friends, I wish I could show you my exulting heart! I am filled with joy when I think of how I have always heard the words, "I am with you to the end of the world," even through long years of waiting in darkness. Such a piece of the world, that weighs one down like a great log on one's shoulders and makes one groan and moan, will fall in its own time; it will come to an end. All the things that torment you, that weigh upon you, that are dark and heavy, come to an end. All the dark powers that we don't understand, though we often sense them; all the restlessness that wants to enter our hearts so that we have to sigh — all this will have an end.

In Jesus all things have an end that are not of God our Father. In His presence we are placed into eternity. In reality our earthly years mean nothing; they are a human concept based on the fact that the earth turns around the sun in a certain way. Now it is outside of time, it is in eternity, that we have come to feel at home with the Lord Jesus. He dwells among us; we dwell with Him. Thus we have been lifted out of the chance happenings of time and into the blessedness of eternity. In the power and in the light of this eternity, in its liberating, redeeming nature, all things that are not of God must have an end.

Wherever there is an end, there is also a new beginning. Many times we want something to happen for God's kingdom. We would like to ask God, "Give this anew; make that new!" Very well, but first you must wait until the old has come to an end. Unless the old comes to an end, there can be nothing new in your heart, in your house, in your whole being. This very fact has comforted me, too, about our life and about our house, which has stood for so many years and where God's kingdom has been prayed for so much.

If something new is to come, something old must first come to an end. And until this end comes we must be patient. We must hold out and say again and again, "He is with us; therefore the end will come!" This is part of our work in faith, in love and in hope. All the hatred in the world, all the vanity of the world, all the wrongness of human thinking and speaking, will come to an end. The end will come soon. Soon the years will come when the darkness will have to flee. Soon the time will come, indeed it is already here, when new feelings come to life in men's hearts. Then they will feel drawn more strongly to what is good. Then our spirit will see more clearly what dark powers still surround us, what the powers are that we do not want. A new will has to come and will come, a will that says, "We no longer want to live for corruption. We no longer want to live for sin. We will not!" Such a time will come, and then all that was corrupt and spoiled will come to an end.

In this way, going forward step by step, we shall reach the great end. It will not come all at once. It will come very quietly. One thing after another will come to an end in the world. One thing after another will no longer be tolerated. You can hardly imagine how great are the powers of God that can give men a new mind and a new heart, so that they themselves will get rid of all that stands in the way. Let us continue confidently on our way, through all our days, at the side of the Savior. The way leads onward, onward into a new time. It leads over and above all that we now see spoiled and ruined. The old world comes to an end. Already a new world lies before our eyes. Out of this new world Jesus Christ speaks to us those words which carry a greater significance today than at any other time, "Behold, I am with you all through the days that are coming, until the end of the world!"

17
OUR HUMAN RIGHT

> And he told them a parable, to the effect that they ought always to pray and not lose heart. He said, "In a certain city there was a judge who neither feared God nor regarded man; and there was a widow in that city who kept coming to him and saying, 'Vindicate me against my adversary.' For a while he refused; but afterward he said to himself, 'Though I fear neither God nor regard man, yet because this widow bothers me, I will vindicate her, or she will wear me out by her continual coming.'" And the Lord said, "Hear what the unrighteous judge says. And will not God vindicate his elect, who cry to him day and night? Will he delay long over them? I tell you, he will vindicate them speedily. Nevertheless, when the Son of man comes, will he find faith on earth?"
> —Luke 18, 1-8

The nearer we come to making our will one with God's will, the more disquieted we become. Indeed, we might almost say that we feel robbed of something to which we have a legitimate right. For it is strange that when we know ourselves to be one with God's will, this does not mean that we are now expected to work for some future good. On the contrary, we feel that we have already received something which is rightfully ours. It has almost become our personal possession, and we are afraid it may be taken from us again. It has thus become a very personal matter for each of us. It is our legitimate right that we should no longer be robbed. Moreover, what we feel in our hearts as God's will should not only be preserved in us; we should also be able to declare it to the whole world. Such indeed is the true right of man.

This right shall not perish in corruption and sin. Instead, a power shall arise out of it which will preserve us in the midst of the bereavements which are yet in store for us. For we are surrounded by robbers who want to rob us of the very best we have. They want to push us down into the common sphere of human life where nothing but vanity determines man's ways. They want to insult and mock us because we seek the higher good. Yet we tell them that we do not merely seek it, but that we have it firmly established in our hearts. It is our right through the will of God, who sent the Savior, and who impressed into our hearts the image of God's true life and justice. If we possess this, what does the rest of the world matter? The world has no right to take this possession from us.

Therefore we need not be shy or timid. People may say to us, "Whatever do you mean with your new kingdom, new conditions, a new justice, new eternal life? What are you after? You have no right to expect anything. The world has always been as it is. You can never change it, do what you will, and we won't let you." Without any hesitation or shyness we may come before the throne of justice, before Him who has the power over heaven and earth and say, "Save us from such nonsense. For many thousands of years men have done their fleeting and unjust works on earth. This way of thinking has taken such a hold of people that they are unable to think in any other way. But what does it matter? Save us from this enemy! The truth is not contained in the history of an unhappy human race burdened with misery, injustice and sin. That is not the truth! Truth is the eternal life and justice of God. Therefore away with everything else! Save us, Father in heaven, and give the victory to the truth of life."

It has indeed become a very personal matter for our hearts. We are like the widow who is concerned for her possessions, as any woman would who no longer finds protection because of human injustice. We must take our cause to the righteous judge. Thanks be to God that the righteous judge is near at hand, so that we can see Him. Even in the midst of unjust mankind, wherever there is justice and righteousness it will not be hidden from us. We can see very clearly what justice is, and we will not renounce it. God's love and mercy and God's life in our human nature — these are our legitimate right. Eternal life is our right. This we ought to see clearly and allow no one to take it from us. We trust and rely at all times upon the Judge who has betrothed himself to us. Indeed, He has made a covenant with us, a promise for a time when we shall be saved from all the evil that still surrounds us.

It is significant in our text that the Lord Jesus looks far ahead into a future when God's will for men shall be fulfilled. This is expressed by the words, "Do you think that when the Son of man is to come, He who represents the eternal human, He who wants to bring us back to God — do you think that He will find faith on the earth? Yes, for as long as there is one true Man, one who stands above all the others, we have faith in Him. We rejoice in His life, in His company, in the fact that He speaks to us and that we can draw near to Him in a personal way.

However, the Lord Jesus does not expect to be on the earth at the time when the widow cries out, "Vindicate me, save me from my adversary!" Can we still place our trust in someone who is no longer among us? Even the disciples of Jesus were tempted. They had placed their full trust in the one who lived among them. Yet when He said He would soon come into the last fight and would lose His life at the hands of His enemies, they protested, "No, that is impossible. Everything will stop once you are no longer among us!" Nevertheless, we must cling to Him even though He is no longer on the earth. Our striving in God's name, the submission of our hearts to God's will, need not suffer from the fact that we can no longer see Him. We must cling to Him.

Yet after centuries of human progress, indeed after two thousand years, will men still place their hopes in this same Jesus? Will men still expect the word of judgment in His name? Will they still expect that through His person those things for which we long will come? Will they still have faith? Does anyone today believe in Jesus Christ as he should? Nowadays people complain and protest that they no longer quite know what to do about God's kingdom or about the gospel — everywhere other voices are heard. Will those who do not want to let this faith be taken from them — will they, can they still believe?

Indeed, my friends, this is no easy matter. It is not so difficult to think a little of Jesus as He was in His own time, the Jesus about whom we read in the Bible, though even in this many people are shaky. Yet even the believers find it almost too difficult to believe in Him as the one on whom everything depends, to believe in Him as a living person. They have been taught that He is no longer on the earth. So they lack the living faith which says, "Whenever I think of Jesus I am filled with awe, in the certainty of His power and glory to the honor of God the Father." Do we feel this awe? We can only feel it with regard to a personal being. We can only feel it if we put an end to our indifferent chatter and to our investigations about the Lord Jesus as though He were something dead. We can feel this awe only if in our hearts the knowledge lives that He is, was and is coming, that He will be. Do we have this faith?

Everything will depend on this faith. Outside of Jesus' person there is nothing to kindle a light in our hearts, nothing to support our hope for the future of mankind. When the image of Jesus Christ departs from your hearts, when the truly living and abiding presence of the Lord Jesus is lost, the light of hope is extinguished. We can have no hope for the world without the person of Jesus Christ. We cannot simply have some vague thoughts about God, some nebulous image of Him. It is not true, as some think, that mankind will automatically develop to a state of perfection, that our earthly conditions can produce something good. It is not true that our hearts can find a way out of the confusion, out of our sin, out of our darkness and wrongdoing. It would be false to imagine that we can achieve something real and true without a faith in Jesus Christ. There is not a single reasonable thought in the whole world with regard to the future of mankind, except what has come through Jesus Christ. Those who say, "We must honor His memory as a historical personality," are under an illusion. In the end they will perish miserably. Nothing will be achieved without the Lord, the Savior of individual man and of all mankind. You may have set your mind on doing all sorts of things to improve the human race in our time. Where did you get such ideas from? You want to do it in a worldly way. Yet your desire springs from the person of Jesus, from nowhere else. Therefore I tell you boldly, we cannot really achieve anything humanly great without believing in the Son of man, in the Lord Jesus.

But do you think that even a few people have this faith? That even only a few feel in an immediate way the presence of Jesus in God's almighty name? Do even a few have this perseverance, this praying without ceasing, without fainting? Only through a living contact and relationship with the Lord Jesus can we come to this praying without ceasing for the divine things, for the divine growth intended for man. Those who remain in a vague and general religion, those who want to get along with human thinking alone, soon become tired and lifeless. They have no real image before their eyes.

Let me give an example of this praying without ceasing. It is so very important even in those earthly things where man is meant to advance. Not so long ago, a few decades perhaps, we saw only lightning in the sky. We talked about electricity. Some people began to ponder about this strange power. It did not leave them in peace. They kept thinking, "Who knows, it might be given into the hands of men. Could not this play of the clouds, this faraway, deadly, terrible yet powerful thing, come into the hands of men?" I remember how millions laughed. Only very few people believed it and did not cease to think about it. And suddenly there it was.

Something like this happens when we see Jesus. Anyone who has an image of Jesus from the Bible, perhaps even through experiences in his own heart, recognizes in Him the powers we need. At first these powers are very far away. They are heavenly powers, great and divine powers. They are so great that today we can hardly understand the life of Jesus in a human, natural way. Yet we do see in Him the mighty powers of God. We look up and think, "Is it possible that these powers will one day become man's possession?"

Let me repeat that without Jesus there can be no improvement for men. In other words, without these powers which we recognize in Him we can achieve nothing. It is just as it was with the lightning which we saw but could not use. Yet nowadays its power runs through the whole world, with and without wires. With this power of lightning our words run everywhere through the air. In a similar way we see God's powers, the divine powers. We can cling to them only with our thoughts. Yet in the living person of Jesus we see these divine powers unfold in a very real way. Thus they have become something earthly. To this very day we can see them and recognize them.

We could of course shake our heads and say that we don't believe it. Yet we, who are like the widow, have a claim to this divine power. This is our possession. This power of God in Jesus Christ shall triumph among men. It is our legitimate right. Therefore we believe and come daily before God saying, "They want to rob us, but please do not let them! We appeal to you. Even if there are only a very few of us, we appeal to you in the name of all men. We appeal to you in the name of the foolish and the clever, the godless and the just. In the name of all men whom you have created for a high purpose we maintain firmly that this power, revealed in Jesus Christ as a power of God, a power of life, is our possession! There is little we can do with it today, for we are attacked and opposed from all sides. We want to hold on to it in quiet. It is our right, our human right. Father in heaven, save us from our adversary!"

There are many who uphold a hope for the future, and although their thinking may be Christian, they have trouble keeping the adversary out of their hearts. With arts and sciences, with all our human thinking, the adversary wants to rob us of the little flame in our hearts. I beg you, my friends, do not believe in such things! Be quite certain that everything we men need has been revealed in Jesus Christ, in His words and deeds.

Where else are we to turn to overcome sin, if not to this judging forgiveness which came to us in Jesus Christ? How else can we fight against evil, if not with this clarity of the living power which shall one day illumine even our bodies? How are we to come unscathed through all the chaos among men, unless the peace revealed through Jesus Christ enters into our hearts, this peace which Jesus proclaimed even in the presence of His enemies? How can we stand above the human turmoil and conflict unless our hearts are moved by the divine purpose? How can we hope to triumph over our own hearts, let alone over all that surrounds us? For this reason we constantly pray, "Save us from our adversary!"

The vision is clearly before our eyes and we say, as people did in earlier times looking at the lightning, "This power must come into the hands of men." Looking at Jesus Christ we say, "This power will be given in rich abundance to those who proclaim the kingdom of God on earth!" Give up your dull and insipid

Christianity; it makes little difference. But do not let Christ be taken from you!

Everything depends on Him. In Him we can really unite. I still have hope that Christians will be able to unite again. If our hearts are filled with His being, what does it matter whether one is Catholic or Protestant. If the vision of Jesus Christ enters into the hearts of those who think at all about God's kingdom, then everything else will fade into the background. The outward differences of our religious practices need not separate us. The one little flame lit in our hearts, the living, powerful kingdom of the future, revealed in the person of Jesus Christ — this is what unites me with people elsewhere, who may be living in other ways and under different circumstances. In this way there will perhaps one day grow a united flock of Jesus Christ, of which it will then be said, **"One** shepherd, **one** flock!"

To anyone who tries to grasp this, it is a bewildering thought. In fact, it is impossible to grasp it with human thoughts. Thousands will tell us, "This will never happen!" Then we must pray and not falter. Who can endure? Who can pray and not falter? Who can seek this highest goal without fear, without worry? Who can remain steadfast and say, "Because it was, it will be," and then add, "And so it is now!" I have not yet met the man who, having constantly prayed for God's will to happen, has not experienced salvation in small things. "He will vindicate them speedily." Do you think I stand before you as one who only expects salvation in the distant future? No.

I too am one of you, one of those who have experienced the truth of the words, "I will vindicate you speedily." This has been so especially at times when I thought I could not go on, when hostility and opposition became so strong that I felt very weak. Then I heard the words, "I will vindicate you speedily."

Everything that will happen in the future must be felt and noticed beforehand by certain people. There is nothing that belongs only to the future. Everything that one day will come in a big way for the whole world, for the whole of mankind, must come first in a small way. All the great things which are to come, we shall already experience today quite certainly in all their glory if we pray and do not falter. But without prayer they will not come. We must have the great cause constantly and firmly before the inner eyes of our hearts. Otherwise we shall be looking to the right and to the left, above and below; our curious eyes will wander all over the world, but we shall miss the main thing. We seek this and that, try to change this or that, and thus do not perceive the true power which is already at work.

This power is discovered only by those who truly look for it. Therefore, let me repeat, do not be like people who grope with a long stick in the dark, but look toward the divine power which appeared in Jesus Christ. Be thankful for any, even the smallest experience you may have of this glory of God in the flesh. Let us not be indifferent about small experiences; such indifference creates nothing but complaint and discontent. We should hold on to the small experiences which teach us the truth contained in the words, "He will vindicate them speedily." Start with the small things. Start in the depth of your own heart! The darkness is still widespread, but something has begun. We in the Spirit may consider ourselves saved, even though there is still much darkness around us.

Do you think the Son of Man will find faith in our time? My friends, I know well how difficult it is. With all our studying and investigating we have clogged up our hearts and heads to the point where we can no longer feel the immediate presence of Jesus Christ. Be that as it may, I do not want the Lord Jesus to be defeated. I still wish that there may be some who look to Him, who pray and do not waver. Even if it were only a few, it would not matter. Maybe only one, maybe a few people, will come into God's kingdom, and soon all will have it. Think of how a fort is taken. One soldier gets there first, others follow, and soon the fort is won. Many times the most important events do not happen through the masses, but through an individual, through a few.

Blessed are we if we prove ourselves as the few. Blessed are we if we can come together as the few in this praying without ceasing. We want to do this because we have felt the greatness of Jesus Christ, our Lord, to whom belongs the victory today and tomorrow as also in the past. He has always been the victor over the dust. Jesus Christ, the image of that which mankind is to be, is before us in radiance and glory. All who open their hearts to God's Spirit can see Him.

18

THE SAVIOR IS COMING!

But of that day and hour no one knows, not even the angels of heaven, nor the Son, but the Father only. As were the days of Noah, so will be the coming of the Son of man. For as in those days before the flood they were eating and drinking, marrying and giving in marriage, until the day when Noah entered the ark, and they did not know until the flood came and swept them all away, so will be the coming of the Son of man. Then two men will be in the field; one is taken and one is left. Two women will be grinding at the mill; one is taken and one is left. Watch therefore, for you do not know on what day your Lord is coming.

—Matthew 24, 36-42

Many times the Savior calls out to us, "Watch!" Here the call is especially to "watch for my coming, for the future of Jesus Christ!" With this call the Lord Jesus gives us a task. It is a blessed, an important task. If we fulfil this task, to watch for His future, it is as though His future were coming into our present time. By our watching we will always have the future before our eyes. The future comes closer. It makes itself felt in our whole nature, in our whole life. We cannot be swallowed up by the present, for we are bound to the future. We experience the future already in our time. Again and again new life is given. Again and again something new develops, something that opens up a way on which we can go. Each time it is a piece of Jesus Christ's future.

THE SAVIOR IS COMING

Christ's future is not one single point in an absolute remoteness for which we are to wait. This is hardly thinkable, for we would probably all go to sleep over it. The future is already present. It must become an experience of Christianity, of every individual Christian. God's deed through Jesus Christ must be your experience, today and tomorrow and every day.

The Savior is coming. He is not quietly sitting somewhere in eternity, waiting for a certain moment when He will suddenly plunge in. He is on the way. We may at all times have His future before our eyes. We may expect it every day. The coming of the Savior runs through Christian history, through God's working in the world, like a thread. If this thread is not to break, the Lord Jesus must ever be coming. Often there will be times of storm and thunder, of sorrow and suffering. Yet in all such storms, in all sorrow, at all times when we think we cannot go on, there will be new ways. New revelations will enable us to continue working and watching. There will come a time when our waiting and watching, which at all times has prepared the coming of the Lord Jesus, will be consummated.

So then, watch, you Christian. Watch, and be joyful. Even though fear may overcome you, watch. Something of the Savior's future will enter into your life. I have often experienced this in the way I have been led. Many times I have had to say, "There is a way out." Even when I felt I could not go on, God has opened a new way. Then one can continue. Then we have a piece of Jesus Christ's future amongst us. We depend on this coming of the Savior. All our Christian thinking and living comes to life by the very fact that we are allowed to expect such great things, things which will finally lead to true life.

Thus we live constantly in Jesus Christ's future, of which the Savior himself says, "Of that day and hour no one knows." It is as though a new element had come into the development of the world through this future of Jesus Christ. It is as though something new had come into world history, causing a lot of confusion, suffering, temptation, hostility, but at the same time there is hope. In our days there are very large circles of people who hope for the good. They do not think, as the heathens do, that things will just go on and on, and that humanity will not reach any goal. Any hope for improvement, any belief that better days will come for mankind, any striving towards better times, are a proof and a result of this one hope which we Christians firmly express by the words, "The Savior is coming!"

We should and can be ever alert and watchful. Jesus Christ's future has to become your personal experience. Whenever you experience protection and remarkable help, whenever you are led on new ways and see others being led on new ways, you should think, "This is a piece of Jesus Christ's future." There is a special atmosphere in Jesus Christ's future. All kinds of signs, all kinds of proofs of God's help, are visible. However poor we may be, however weak we may feel, we want to continue hoping and watching.

A time will come when you will be allowed to act. That is a piece of Jesus Christ's future.

Yet it remains a mystery of God. God is the mighty power, the tremendous energy which directs human development. Therefore it cannot be determined or foretold, "On such and such a day, at such and such an hour it will come." For then it would seem as though there had been nothing at all before that time. It would appear as though we had nothing to tell about the coming of the Lord Jesus into our lives. Yet we have a lot to tell and should take everything seriously that we experience. This is what watching means. Watch out! Suddenly something happens to you. Then you must grasp it! Then you may live again. Then you must believe. Then seize the good things which the Father in heaven places at your feet.

The Savior is coming! He is on the way to you, to me, to us all, in all circumstances of our lives. Even when things are as they were in Noah's time, even if the whole world apparently is concerned with nothing but earthly things, with eating and drinking, with marrying and giving in marriage, we should not give up. We must be a living element at all times. Our Christianity must be alive. Our Christian faith must be a light, a light of hope, a light in the midst of the indifference of the world and of men. It must be a light even in the midst of all the works of the world. We expect greater things than new machines and inventions. We expect the good in our hearts, in our lives. We expect the overcoming of the powers of evil, of all sin that still prevails. We expect the victory over all the misery that binds so many people, over all the evil and hostile powers that torment men. This is our expectation. It will surpass by far any apparent triumphs which men experience through their own works.

In this expectation we will not become weary. We will not become poor, nor will we become irritable or quarrelsome. We will not be dissatisfied with our conditions and with the events that surround us. In all things we will see the Savior coming.

We too, in all our activities, must live in Jesus Christ's future. The fact that so many things happened in recent times which made it possible for us to carry on, is a piece of Jesus Christ's coming. There are some who complain, who want things to be different, who always think of the good old times and want to have them back. They are quite wrong. They torment themselves and others as well. Even now, certain events or experiences are felt by some to be a help, to be a sign of Jesus Christ's future. Then they thank God and rejoice. Yet others are depressed and think, "Oh dear, I never thought this was possible; it is quite different from what it used to be." Then some will be accepted, that is, they will joyfully and gladly continue on their way in the certainty that the Lord Jesus is coming. The others get nothing out of it and go sadly on their way.

The future of Jesus Christ must become a real eperience in world history, in the history of the church and of Christianity. It must become a reality in the experience of every Christian. Your life must be a piece of Jesus Christ's future, your life and also your death. Our dying should not lead into death but into life. Even in our last moments Jesus Christ's future must touch us. The dying must say, "The Savior is coming!" The sinners, upon their awakening and repenting, must say, "The Savior is coming!" In all our afflictions we should say, "The Savior is coming!" All our troubles and afflictions have something good, something to teach us.

In this way we should be watching. I know of no other way to do it. In our own lives we have to experience His coming. There is a justification in thinking that the Savior is quite near. It is right to say with the apostles, "He is at hand, He will come soon!" He will not only come at some moment which lies in a distant future; our whole life is filled with the coming of the Lord Jesus. Daily we rejoice at His coming. Daily He opens up new ways for us, on which we can carry on joyfully. Daily He opens new doors for us, He helps us and protects us, often without our knowledge. Yet again and again we are allowed to recognize His help when suddenly, like a miracle, we see that we have been protected. This is the Lord Jesus.

Watch and pray, the Lord Jesus is coming! This watching is a part of our life, of our service to God. The Savior urges us seriously to "Watch, watch, watch!" as though He wanted to lay a foundation for it in our hearts, in our whole lives. It is as though He were always waiting and asking, "How can I come closer to this person, to that person? How can I meet this one who is waiting for me? How can I go to meet many at a time, so that again and again new victories are given? What can I do to make the call heard throughout Christendom, throughout the whole world, 'Jesus lives, Jesus is victor!' " For in our watching we think not only of our own lives. We are watching for the whole world. We are thinking of the world which is still in darkness. We lift our hearts and heads, saying, "Father in heaven, the world is yours. You have given us minds and hearts with which to wait and to strive forward. You have made men of us, you who are the God of all gods, the Savior of all men."

In the small circle of a family, of a household, we are watching. Man, watch for yourself! You need it. Do not fall into darkness and indifference, but watch! Your own hour will come — be prepared for it. The hour will come for your inner growth, for the development of your life, for the renewal of your life and of your death. Watch! Never lose heart. The Savior often comes in the most difficult hour, in the most unhappy times. Watch, for the Savior is on the way!

Watch for the world, too. Do not give the world up as though it were lost for all eternity. It is true that Jesus Christ's future brings separation. A judgment lies in the fact that one person can come to faith and to the joy in God, while another remains outside for the time being. But this should not trouble us. The future of Jesus Christ is and will be a great and powerful help in all situations for all men. All eyes will be opened. Then people will weep and wail when they see how wrong they were; but their tears must contain the truth of Jesus Christ's future, of the Savior's coming, if the many are to receive help.

We live in the future of Jesus Christ. Never shall we be able to say that the Savior has not come, that we have experienced nothing of Jesus Christ's future. Just think how much we have been given. How many times we have received help and protection, often very suddenly and unexpectedly. All of a sudden it was here, this future of our Lord Jesus Christ. Let it come to life among us! Let us not just look to the distant future, as though something impossible had to come then. Let it come to life now, in our daily life. Let it come to life in your personal experiences. Let it come to life on your sickbed. For the Savior comes also to the sick, to the poor, to those who have to struggle for their daily bread. The Savior is coming! This certainty is our joy; it is the source of our Christian life. Let us remain in this joyful certainty every day of our lives. Let it fill our days, today and tomorrow. It will not abandon us. The fact that we are allowed to say, "The Savior is coming!" is like a surging tide of God's Spirit. This tide will never end; it will continue to carry us forward, to lead us and bless us in all our thoughts and endeavors, in our whole life.

Therefore watch! Watch, all of you! Let each one be a fighter for Jesus Christ, a servant of the Savior. Give yourselves in and let your hearts be prepared. Then Jesus Christ can come to you, into your house, into your hearts, into your lives. Never forget this: Watch! The Savior is coming!

19

THE NEW REALITY

Can any of you convict me of sin? If not, why is it that you do not believe me when I tell you the truth? The man who belongs to God listens to God's words; it is because you do not belong to God that you will not listen to me. Hereupon the Jews answered him, We are right, surely, in saying that thou art a Samaritan, and art possessed? I am not possessed, Jesus answered; it is because I reverence my Father that you have no reverence for me. Not that I am looking to my own reputation; there is another who will look to it, and be the judge. Believe me when I tell you this; if a man is true to my word, to all eternity he will never see death. And the Jews said to him, Now we are certain that thou art possessed. What of Abraham and the prophets? They are dead; and thou sayest that a man will never taste death to all eternity, if he is true to thy word. Art thou greater than our father Abraham? He is dead, and the prophets are dead. What dost thou claim to be? If I should speak in my own honor, Jesus answered, such honor goes for nothing. Honor must come to me from my Father, from him whom you claim as your God: although you cannot recognize him. But I have knowledge of him; if I should say I have not, I should be what you are, a liar. Yes, I have knowledge of him, and I am true to his word. As for your father Abraham, his heart was proud to see the day of my coming; he saw, and rejoiced to see it. Then the Jews asked him, Hast thou seen Abraham, thou, who art not yet fifty years old? And Jesus said to them, Believe me, before ever Abraham came to be, I am. Whereupon they took up stones to throw at him; but Jesus hid himself, and went out of the temple.   —John 8, 46-59 (Knox)

The truth is at stake. The truth shall be proclaimed by Jesus' whole being, by all He does, by all He says. This truth, which He wants to represent in the world unto the present day, is that He came from God. He came from the almighty, great and mysterious God. He came from the God who creates all things, who has made all things. He came from the God in whose hands lies the development of all things from the beginning of Israel's history, from Abraham's time until His own time. He came from the God who lives in the growth of mankind, in the evolution of the whole world. In God all things awaken again and again to new life, all things tend toward the one glorious goal. This is the God from whom Jesus came. Therefore in Him something new came to the earth.

This truth must become a new reality. It is not a matter of new teachings, new laws, new institutions. True, Christianity has made many teachings and laws and institutions after Jesus. Yet this not the truth we are to hear. The truth to which we are to open our ears is the new message the Son of man brings to the world. It is the message that God now creates a new reality on the earth, at first among men, and later in the whole creation. Heaven and earth will be renewed in this new reality.

We are living in the old reality which completely occupies all our senses. It is the old story of perishing, of wasting away, and behind it lies a mighty darkness: death. We live and die. Nature lives and then dies. Sin enters into life. There are failures; men go on wrong ways. This also is a reality. But it is a reality of misery and suffering. We men were and are expected to defend ourselves against it. Yet we could not. Thus the whole history of mankind became one of dying and, what is more, of death.

In Jesus a new reality appears, a reality which is opposed to that of world history. Something new is to begin alongside the old. The old reality does not suddenly disappear; it continues alongside. Yet in Jesus we have a new reality. A new history begins, a new working of God. True, God was present in the old world, and His Spirit worked upon its growth and development. He did send men who were able to witness to Him. However, it always remained the old reality; the world could not come to anything new. Now, yes now, something new is to begin with Jesus Christ. It was meant to be like that from the very beginning, but death still had a power over men. Even in the lives of believing men, death made itself felt. This death was particularly strong when Jesus appeared, this death caused by the law, this deadliness of human teachings. It was so strong that the Lord Jesus had to struggle greatly in order to make people see that in Him something new had come, a new history.

This new history is to become revealed in each individual person. In you, in myself, in all of us, it must become evident. Now something new is possible. Of course we will have to fight for it day by day. We have to learn to grasp that this fact that Jesus came from God is the truth. All things of which we men have need flow from this one truth. This new fact, that God came to mankind, is the source of all that is needful. We can achieve nothing unless we place ourselves into this new truth. With all our Christian talking and praying, with all our institutions, nothing seems to change. Yet where one man fully accepts this truth which is Christ, there things begin to change. In this new fact of divine history, this beginning of a new history on earth, we experience a change. It is a constant source of renewal, and the greatest possibilities are given in this truth: Christ. This is no dogma; it is not just a new word. It is the word which has miraculous powers. It is the living person of Jesus Christ, in whom dawns a new history of mankind.

This we must believe today more than ever. If we do this, we belong to God. This truth, that Jesus Christ has come from God, must bear fruit. To begin with, you and others, perhaps many, maybe only a few, must become children of God. We have to become children of God, for the Savior says, "Unless one is born anew, he cannot see the kingdom of God." (John 3, 3) The kingdom of heaven stands upon the reality of Jesus Christ's life which has come from God.

Therefore, to this very day we are faced with the question: Are you living in the essence of Jesus Christ? Have you placed yourself under the authority which has been given to Jesus for you and for all men? Can you really grasp this? Can you accept it, can you take it into your life? Can you let this guide your whole life, even in the midst of all the suffering which still remains?

Unless we do this, we shall have no right to strive for the kingdom of God. For what is God's kingdom? Certainly not Christian institutions, although in these too there can be something of God's kingdom. God's kingdom is the power of God; it is the rulership of God. God's kingdom brings the revelation of divine life, the birth of new hearts, new minds, new feelings. Thus we shall be guided onto the right way. This is God's kingdom. Yet who can grasp what it means when God rules? It is almost too great for Christians to grasp, even in our days. Who can grasp what God is at all? What is God in eternity, where He rules and guides the evolution of all things? What is God in the heart of one man? Who is God in your destiny, in what you experience, in what may be hard for you and yet is under God's rule? What is God?

To understand this we must acknowledge that Jesus has come from God. He is the light that shines throughout the centuries since the day of His birth. He is the light which is preserved for us in the gospel. He is the light which opposes the sinfulness that burdens us. He is the light that opposes death. Jesus has come from God to triumph over sin and death. Of Him it could be said, "Can any of you convict me of sin?" Jesus has come from God to triumph over death after the most painful suffering. Jesus Christ has come into our midst as one of us. He has laid the foundation for a completely new life, for a new growth. In Him we can become completely new men in the very depth of our hearts and not just with words. Whoever has recognized the greatness of this truth will be able to find even today the life of which it is said, "Believe me when I tell you this; if a man is true to my word, to all eternity he will never see death."

This is the power, the true nature of God's kingdom. Of what use is our Christianity if we keep falling back into death and if darkness continues to surround our lives? What good is our faith in God if we vanish as though nothing had happened? What use is our faith in Christ if everything goes on in the old ruts? We are in a bad way if the power of sin continues to work in us and the power of death keeps threatening mankind. Then our Christianity, our belief in God, is of little value. Facts must become visible, facts of life, of new life, new strength, new joy. We no longer live under the rulership of death. We no longer live under the power of sin. We are no longer subject merely to misery, although we continue to be miserable creatures. We live in the growth of the true life that comes from God, the true life which the Spirit of Jesus Christ pours out over all mankind throughout the ages.

Although we may often not even notice it, there is a development of true life. It exists parallel to the development of sin, of death; but it is there. Two currents are now running alongside and in opposite directions one to the other. Sin wants to rule, wants to reach a goal. It seems as though its goal were to corrupt men more and more, to prevent them from achieving anything good. Against this current runs the current of Jesus Christ, the Prince of life. He leads us into something completely new, into a new reality. In this new reality we must believe. Since Jesus Christ has come, your evil, even your death, will be overcome. An end must be put to everything that is of death. Even if we still have to die, He has said, "Whoever believes in me shall not see death, even though he die." The outward dying, the passing of our physical life, is not so important. But the death brought about by sin is a heavy matter. The shadow of death, of which the prophet Isaiah already spoke, lies heavy upon us. The shadow of centuries of men's dying, only to perish in this death, weighs upon us. The shadow of the ages, with all that wants to corrupt men unto this very day, is a heavy burden to us. Yet now the great words are spoken, "Whoever keeps my word will no longer see death." I say "no longer," for we have seen death in all its dreadful forms; we have experienced it. Sometimes it comes so close to us that we can feel it almost physically despite our faith. We have seen death, ah, how long! Looking back over the history of mankind, even that of Christianity, we see death, nothing but death. Not just dying, but death. Dying cannot destroy us. Though we die, we shall still live. But once death overcomes us we are paralyzed. All we have ever done is over; death has swallowed it up. Therefore let us hear the new words, "If you are true to my word, you will not see death in all eternity."

What greater words could be said to us? If we can hear these words, then the history of mankind will also be renewed. All those who believe, all those who truly penetrate into the reality of Jesus' life, will no longer see death but pass into eternity like shining lights. Thus a light will also shine on the earth. This light must come from beyond the earth, from heaven. It must come from the place where Jesus Christ now rules and triumphs and judges. A day must break in upon the earth. Yet this day cannot come from the earth; it cannot be brought about by new human thoughts, new inventions or great deeds of men. This new day must come from eternity.

This new day has now dawned for us. It has come into the past and into the future. It is the eternity of Christ, expressed in His words, "Before ever Abraham came to be, I am." Abraham, and Moses too, and the prophets, live in eternity. Yet the eternity in which Jesus Christ lives is a higher eternity, a brighter one, one which penetrates more deeply into our lives. For Jesus Christ is the one who rose from the dead. It is He who matters to us. We do not want to cling to men, not even to the religious, pious people. Everything must come from the ruler, from Jesus Christ. He alone can be victorious. He alone can pierce through all the powers of sin and death. No human being can do it, not even the best teachers will achieve it. Things will remain just as they are until Christ appears. Yet one day the Lord Jesus will be at our side. Then we shall no longer have to look upon the horrors of death and sin. We shall no longer have to see darkness; instead we shall see the light which dawned with Jesus since the day of His birth. Then He will come in His glory, and all men will rejoice in God's kingdom.

Already today we can rejoice in God's kingdom through Christ, in the small things. In little, individual things there are already traces of God's kingdom. Look at your own life. God's kingdom is present also in your life, and you must see it. If you don't see it, then it is as though the Lord were saying to you, "You are not God's child, for you do not see the truth." What is truth in the world? What is truth in our own lives? Only what God does, in us and to us, is truth. Of this truth we shall yet experience a great deal, and we shall experience it together.

I have fellowship with many. I do not want human fellowship, human friendship. I do not want human praise. Yet I rejoice in a certain fellowship with men who acknowledge what God has done in them. To me this is the most important thing of all that concerns my own life. We do have a great fellowship with men who in all things, in all their experiences, say, "How much has the Lord of the kingdom of God already done for me! How much evil has been led to a good end! How often have I been saved from distress, raised up out of fear, made joyful again after I had been sad. How often has God forgiven my sins and wiped out my wrongdoing. How much love has He shown to me! How often have I experienced the reality of a higher authority in my life. How often God has stepped into my life. This has been possible and is now possible through the coming of the Lord Jesus, who has come from God."

Believe me, my friends, everything is different in the world since Jesus came from God and went to God. To all those who come to know Christ, a new possibility is given. Not everything is overcome yet. Indeed, there is much still to be overcome. But there is a new possibility for God to show His mercy to us. God can again rule the world and the lives of individual men. This possibility must live in our hearts. Then the true Christ will be with us, He who came to bring life against death.

Let us therefore be courageous and strong in our own lives. When things are hard to bear, when it becomes difficult and we can hardly escape the snares of death, then let us be watchful. Be strong in the Lord, your Savior! Be strong! He is near! Be strong in the fight and stand firm at the side of the Lord Jesus. A fight is raging in the world today. In this fight we must be faithful and steadfast, every single day. We must not rely on our own strength, on our own possibilities, but only on the eternal Lord and victor, Jesus Christ, who is, was and shall be. Soon God's day will dawn on the earth. Already we can see its first messengers. It will be here before we know it. Then the fight will end in a great victory. Not only your life, not only individual lives, will be renewed when that day comes. The life of all nations will enter into a new history. This is a history which we cannot bring about. It must come from God alone, from the Almighty who rules and triumphs and judges through Jesus Christ in all eternity, until the great goal is attained.

OTHER PUBLICATIONS BY THE PLOUGH PUBLISHING HOUSE

Inner Words for Every Day of the Year, chosen and arranged by Emmy Arnold. Each day brings you a quotation from the writings of both Blumhardts, Dietrich Bonhoeffer, Bodelschwingh, Eberhard Arnold, and others. These men were willing to put into daily practice what they believed, regardless of the consequences. 1963. 188 pp. Price $3.00. Cloth bound.

The Secret Flower, a story by Jane T. Clement taking place in the England of the Middle Ages. This story documents the awakening and groping of one medieval business man toward the land of the "secret flower." 1961. 64 pp. Price $1.25. Paper bound.

Joy in the Lord, a talk given by Christoph Blumhardt on Christmas Eve, 1899, in Bad Boll, Germany. Blumhardt speaks of his longing that men gather together to live for God's kingdom on earth. 1963. 16 pp. Price 30¢.

Children in Community, a photographic essay written and selected by the teachers and children of the Society of Brothers. Over 70 photographs. Much writing and drawing by children. Articles on child training by Eberhard Arnold and others. Now in preparation. Price $3.00. Hard bound cover.

The Hour and its Challenge, by Eberhard Arnold. This pamphlet is concerned with the question of peace. How can a man find peace? How much time is yet allowed him? Re-edited 1961. 11 pp. Price 20¢.

The Peace of God, by Eberhard Arnold. This book translates a chapter of *Innenland: a Guide into the Soul of the Bible*. Also includes a brief introduction to the author's life and work. 1940. 96 pp. Price $1.50. Paper bound.

The Early Christians, by Eberhard Arnold. The author shares his deep understanding of Christ's followers from the time of the death of the apostles until about 180 A.D. 1939. 124 pp. Price $1.75. Paper bound.

Order from
THE PLOUGH PUBLISHING HOUSE
Rifton, New York